CULTIVATING YOUR *it* FACTOR

*14 Must Haves To Discover,
Define and Refine Your Signature Brand*

A Collaboration Presented By

STEVII AISHA MILLS, MS

Copyright © 2015 Stevii A. Mills

All rights reserved. No part of this book may be reproduced, distributed or transmitted in any form by any means, graphics, electronics, or mechanical, including photocopy, recording, taping, or by any information storage or retrieval system, without permission in writing from the publisher, except in the case of reprints in the context of reviews, quotes, or references.

Scriptures marked NIV are taken from the Holy Bible, *New International Version®*, NIV®. Copyright © 1973, 1978, 1984, 2011 by Biblica, Inc.™. All rights reserved.

Scriptures marked NKJV are taken from the Holy Bible, *New King James Version®*, NKJV®. Copyright © 1982 by Thomas Nelson. All rights reserved.

Scriptures marked AMP are taken from the Holy Bible, *Amplified Version®*, AMP®. Copyright © 1954, 1958, 1962, 1964, 1965, 1987 by Zondervan®. All rights reserved.

Scriptures marked KJV are taken from the Holy Bible, *King James Version®*, KJV®. Copyright © 1982 by Thomas Nelson, Inc. All rights reserved.

Scriptures marked NLT are taken from the Holy Bible, *New Living Translation Version®*, Copyright © 1996, 2004, 2007, 2013 by Tyndale House Foundation. All rights reserved.

Published by: Purposely Created Publishing Group™
Printed in the United States of America

ISBN-10: 1-942-83823-9
ISBN-13: 978-1-942838-23-4

Special discounts are available on bulk quantity purchases by book clubs, associations and special interest groups. For details email: sales@publishyourgift.com
or call (888) 949-6228.

For information logon to:
www.PublishYourGift.com

Table of Contents ...

Acknowledgments	v
Foreword	xi
Introduction	xv

Must Have Principles

1. **God Given It Factor #GGIF** — 1
   Stevii Aisha Mills
2. **Spirituality** — 15
   Verna V. Nickelberry
3. **Authentic Identity** — 25
   Debrayta (Dee) Salley
4. **Soul Nourishment** — 37
   M.E. Porter
5. **Courage** — 49
   Fungai Ndemera
6. **Tenacity** — 63
   Rhonda McAlister
7. **Value Awareness** — 75
   Fungai Ndemera
8. **Money Management** — 89
   Lisa Wilson
9. **Lifestyle Balance** — 103
   Minister Nellie Wosu

10	**Stress Relief** Miste M. Anders-Clemons	111
11	**Healthy Self-Concept** Alaina Odessa	125
12	**Signature Presence** Cherri Walston	141
13	**Leverage IQ** Famira M. Green	151
14	**Time Management** Toneika Sherrod	163
About the Authors		175

Acknowledgements •••

This book is dedicated to:

Karen Mills, Mom, you have always been the wind beneath my wings. You have sacrificed so much for me, and for that I thank you. You have not only been a dynamic mother; you have been my very best friend, my twin, and my heart. May you know that I will always do my best to show the world what you planted within me.

Fred Mills, Daddy, you are so special to me. You showed me how to fearlessly live my dream. As I am writing, we celebrate your 50 years in music and your 30 years with Sweet Dreams Band! Wow! That is remarkable. It shows love, talent, dedication, and power. I love you to life!

Laurene Wise Mills, I miss you more than words can say, but I experience your love daily. You are a true blessing to me, and I thank you for leaving a legacy that is a strong blueprint for all women to follow. I love you always.

The Mills Family (and all of our relatives), there are so many of us, and naming each one name by name would make up an entire book. Just know that I am thankful for each and every one of you and for the amazing impact that you have had on my life.

Faye Muse, Betty Allford, and Michael Allford, I love you and appreciate all the fun and lessons that I have learned from you.

The Mason Family, thank you for teaching me about family, faith, and education. You all are absolutely amazing.

Danny Clay, I have learned so much from you. You lead and live by example. The music is truly the magnificence. You are so amazing! Your life is truly counting for something.

Danielle, you are indeed my sister. Thank you for being part of the greatest memories that I have had from our teens, college years, and now adulthood. All I have to say is... get ready, Gayle!

North Carolina A&T State University, you shaped me into the woman that I am today and taught me a lot in and out of the classroom. Thank you for all of the lessons that I have learned. Aggie Pride!

Pastors Lee and Shonia Stokes & Destiny Christian Center, thank you for allowing me to serve in the house for the past 11 years and counting. I have learned so much about me and my destiny just by being connected. I love my DCC family!

Maurice & Lashonda Stokes, you two are a blessing to me. I am so blessed to be connected and to know people who are truly stronger than their circumstances and who have continually loved each other to infinity and beyond.

Robyn Gaskins Smith, thank you for bringing the brand to life. You are a blessing to me, and your heart is amazing. You saw the "It Factor" in me before there were even words to describe it.

Mike Looney, CUZ!! I love you! Thank you for seeing the possibilities and cheering for me all the way! You are a blessing! Keep doing grand things!

Tamyka Washington, thank you for being my #PowerPartner. You are a gift to this world, and so many people are blessed by just seeing you on your journey. Continue to do amazing things and #WOW them.

Michelle Washington, thank you for being a great friend and other mother. I love you!

Mista Parle, every time I listen to the Just Stevii song, it blesses me. Thank you for using your It Factor and putting words to my brand! You are amazing!

Gareth & Linease Washington, you are phenomenal! Thank you for all that you do and all that you are! Many blessings! I love you both!

Alicia "Luv Lee" Diggs, There are many people who come for a reason or a season. Thank you my sister for being here for a lifetime. You have an amazing story to tell and I cannot wait to see it written on the pages.

Carina Cole, Thank you for showing me how to rock my brand image before I even knew what it was! You are a blessing! I love you my sister.

Raymond and Kim Larkin, Thank you for your pure hearts and real love. Red carpets are calling!

The Chic Shepreneurs everywhere, continue to follow your heart and rock your #GGIF. Your dream is amazing, and it deserves to live.

Dawniel Winningham, thank you for writing our foreword and for just being a dynamic, shining example of a Chic Shepreneur. I appreciate you.

Fungai, Marilyn, Cyneta, Cherri, Alaina, Famira, Lisa, Debrayta, Nellie, Verna, Miste, Rhonda, Toneika, you all are simply remarkable. Thank you for seeing my vision and running with it. Thank you for investing your time, finances, effort, energy, words, and hearts into the pages of this book. I could not have done it without each and every one of you. You all are blessings! Love you lots!

Tieshena Davis & Purposely Created Publishing, thank you for your dedication and your work in bringing this project to life. Your whole team is amazing and ultra-professional! Continue to rock your #GGIF

Anyone else who has truly ever encouraged and supported me, I appreciate you, and I honor you with this book. You mean a lot to me and help us all continue on this journey in life! Many blessings!

Foreword

By Dawniel Winningham

For the most part, I always knew what "IT" was. There were many things that made me avoid "IT." Fear was a major contributing factor, along with not knowing how to grow "it" or build "it." For quite some time I ignored "it" and tried to deny "it"; but after a while, "it" was undeniable.

When I say "it," I am referring to my destiny, my purpose—that thing I was put on Earth by the most high to accomplish. Truth be told, you probably know what your "it" is as well. You may not be crystal clear on how you are supposed to use it to serve the world with it just yet, but you have some clue as to how you are supposed to be using "it."

I often tell people that I am still on the potter's wheel. What I mean is that GOD is constantly using my experiences in the world, things I learn, and the people I meet to shape my message and purpose. The things in life that I feel have hurt me are, in retrospect, more often than not, the very things that allowed me to become who I am.

The same is true for you even if you have yet to realize it. This type of cultivation is often unintentional; however, it plays a major role in moving you towards your purpose.

Now, what Stevii and the other authors have outlined for you are things that YOU can do to move even quicker towards your purpose. I say "purpose" because upon discovering the purpose you were put on the earth, you will realize your greatest success.

While success is not a straight line, and there is no direct path to get there, no foolproof blueprint, what Stevii outlines is essential if you want to be successful. They must be done and must be completed in order for you to claim and refine your "it" factor. Almost like an apprenticeship, these must be learned prior to you being able to claim that you are the master.

There are two things that will happen when you begin this journey, and if you are reading this I must assume that you are ready to begin.

Cultivating Your IT Factor

The first is that you will CONSTANTLY feel a sense of fear and dread as you realize what you must sacrifice in order to live your "it" factor. The second is that the closer you become to identifying your "it" factor, the better you will feel about your entire life and reason for being on this planet.

So, while this is a difficult choice, it is a choice that YOU alone will be able to make, and that YOU alone MUST make in order to move forward. You have to decide which you want MOST: a life that YOU are comfortable with, or a LIFE that you were BORN to LIVE! And realize that while you make this choice, it is a choice that not only impacts you, but the many in the world you were placed here to be of service to.

Now focus, move FORWARD, and go for "it."

With Love,

Dawniel Patterson Winningham

Award-Winning Master Business Coach
International Speaker
Bestselling Author

www.iAmDawnielWinningham.com

Introduction

Your God Given It Factor (GGIF) is the "secret sauce" that only you have. It is your gifts, skills, talents, and abilities. It is your *vada va voom* and your *je ne sais quoi*. They all come together, mixing and blending to create the dynamic person that we call YOU.

Our book, *Cultivating Your It Factor*, serves as a handbook that we want you to hold close to you as you journey through life and create your signature brand. There are two definitions for the word cultivate:

1) preparing and using (land) for crops or gardening;

2) trying to acquire or develop (a quality, sentiment, or skill).

The authors of this book have sown our words, our directions, our mistakes and more into its pages so we can prepare you for your dynamic success. Thank you for serving as our garden!

Cultivating Your IT Factor

You are now on the path to acquiring and developing. The beauty of this is that you soon will be on the side of being the cultivator, and you will be able to sow into your own beautiful garden of people to whom God has called YOU to serve.

1

Must Have Principle:

God Given It Factor #GGIF

STEVII AISHA MILLS

In order to truly discover, define, and refine your signature brand, you must holistically get to the bottom of who you are. This journey begins with determining who you are not, so that you can live freely in who you are.

You are not your circumstances. You are not your mistakes. You are not what people have called you. You are not the negative adjectives that you have thought about or called yourself.

1. You are who God calls you to be.

2. You are who you call yourself to be.

3. You are what you are called to do.

First, let's talk about what God calls you.

Jeremiah 1: 5 (NIV Version)

"Before I formed you in the womb I knew you, before you were born I set you apart; I appointed you as a prophet to the nations."

Ephesians 2:10 (Amplified Version)

10 For we are God's [own] handiwork (His workmanship), [a]recreated in Christ Jesus, [born anew] that we may do those good works which God predestined (planned beforehand) for us [taking paths which He prepared ahead of time], that we should walk in them [living the good life which He prearranged and made ready for us to live].

Let's break down these verses.

In Jeremiah, we find out that, whether your mother and father planned for you or not, you were planned. God, who is the King of Kings and the Lord of Lords, took His time to intricately create you. Some of what He knew, that He wanted to put in your #GGIF, may have been your gift of knowing exactly what to say to make everyone laugh, or your ability to design amazing graphics, or maybe even your ability to keep the dance floor jumping all night long. No one can do you like you can do you.

Wow!

Do you know how important you are?

Don't worry, I did not know either.

That is why we are here to talk about your #GGIF.

The verse that we have in Ephesians lets us know that we are custom designed by the most dynamic designer to ever exist. When we think of custom-designed clothing, we know that these are clothes that are created to specifically fit you. They are not off of the rack.

That is how God created you. Even if you are in an industry full of people who do the same thing as you, you are still custom designed!

Think about it: I am sure that if I ask you to recommend a lawyer, you will be able to name the lawyer who stands out to you. What about a doctor?

What about your favorite teacher? Those who stand out most are those who made a dynamic impact on your life. This is what your #GGIF is all about. It is all about blinging out your brand with the things that only you possess.

Think about identical twins. They may look alike, but they are different. Even if their difference is slight, it is still a difference. No two people on this planet are the same, have ever been the same, or will ever be the same. How amazing is that? I am excited about that because it shows how important you are to God. He created you right now for the purpose that he planted inside of you. He could have created you in the prehistoric age or even in the space age.

Instead, he divinely chose you for this age. Then He put more icing on the cake by creating those who are assigned to you and those who you are assigned to in this age, too. Everything that God does is strategic.

People who are assigned to you are people who cannot fulfill their purpose unless you fulfill yours. Yes, it is a high charge to have on your life. However, God created us all for purpose and relationship. Many of us have heard of the word "tribe." Your tribe has been set apart for you. If you do not do what God has called you to do, then your tribe will not move. No matter how big or small this group of people is, they are assigned to you. I will tell you right now that if you do not do what you are purposed to do, you are being selfish. Why? Because there are people praying for an answer to their questions and their problems. God has planted that answer in you. He may have put it in the way you create hair designs. He may have created it in the way you raise your children. He may have created it in the song you sing.

Only you know what God has been nudging you to do. Spend time having meetings with Him. The only way to determine something's purpose is to ask its creator. Our creator is our heavenly father. Your purpose is found in what you love to do. It is what you do effortlessly. It is what people keep coming to you for and asking you to do. It is the thing that God gives you energy to do. It is what sets your soul on fire and sends bolts of electricity through your veins. It is what you must give yourself permission to do.

Those assigned to you are your mentors. Thus, it is imperative that you find people whom you trust and who are doing what you desire to do. These people will take you under their wings, and they will assist you. They can be mentors who are assigned to you whom you know personally, and whom you may find on social media platforms, in books, or in magazines. They have the words that will unlock the keys to your future. They open the doors of your mind so that you can be elevated to your next level of greatness. They are the ones whom you can trust to hold you accountable so you can be even more successful and sharper than you have ever imagined yourself to be.

● ● ● ● ● ●

I have had several mentors over the years, and each of them has imparted great wisdom into my life. They have introduced me to another way of thinking. Just think, what if they did not tap into their #GGIF? You would not be here today reading my book. Why? Because I would not have had the foresight or the courage to believe that I could write a book. That is why I know that it is imperative for you to depart from the Sea of Sameness and the Meadows of Mediocrity. Someone is waiting on you because you have their answers.

I remember when I was not sure of my purpose and what I needed to do to even begin thinking of my purpose. I was blessed to be able to see other people living their purpose and living in their dream. I knew that I wanted that for myself, so I began to connect with them and listen to them. I have notebooks upon notebooks of nuggets that they have shared with me, showing exactly how they did what they did. I did not mind investing in myself because I knew that I wanted what they had. Even when I did not have two pennies to rub together, I knew that I had to figure out a way to gain their knowledge.

I began connecting with their teleseminars and webinars. I was totally transparent, letting them know that I was unable to pay full price, but that I could pay some money. I let them know what I wanted to do with my life, and guess what happened? They took me under their wings and mentored me. They took their time to cultivate me, and now, because of their assistance, I can cultivate you. No matter if the mentorship was short-term or long-term, I was able to learn and grow. I still hold on to the knowledge that they imparted in me. If none of us tapped into our #GGIF, the spark within us would never get out. It would indeed die. You must feed the spark inside of you so that it can grow into a blaze.

As we look further into what we call ourselves, we must look beyond the mirror. We see a reflection, but not one that eyes can see. It is a reflection of your heart, mind, spirit, and soul. If you are in divine alignment, then you will be able to see yourself as God sees you.

If you are not, then it will be harder for you to see who He has custom designed you to be. The amazing thing is that the gifts, skills, talents, and abilities that are created inside you are the same, whether you see yourself as God sees you or not. Wow! Reread that sentence and let it sink in. You were created for a specific reason. It is up to you to bring that reason to life.

In order for you to make that happen, you must envision it first. You must see it in your mind. The way I learned how to do that is to first envision who I desired to be. I mean in every way. I imagined what I would eat, what I would be doing professionally, who I would be friends with, who I would be married to, where I would live, where I would travel, and more! I thought of every detail. I wanted to have my vision absolutely crystal clear so I could see it whenever I thought of it.

When I had hard times, I thought of it. When I got excited, I thought of it. All of the time. In fact, I am still thinking of it. It is my mind movie.

The Bible talks about being transformed by the renewing of your mind. I submit to you that in order to truly get to wherever you desire to be in life, you must have your mind opened to receive what you desire. You cannot do it by listening to the negative noise that plays in your mind over and over again. You cannot do it by being around negative people. I believe that people fall into two categories in life: basement people and balcony people.

Basement people are the ones who are always tearing you down. They are often the ones who are upset and angry because they see you succeeding, but they do not believe that they can succeed. The balcony people are ones who are lifting you up. They are your mentors, supporters, and cheerleaders. Our job is to make sure that balcony people outweigh the basement people in our lives. Sometimes the people who are the most negative in our lives are those with the same last name as ours. Yes, some people have family members that are extremely negative. Normally, they do not mean to be negative. They think that they are protecting you from getting hurt.

These are the people who tell entrepreneurs to get a job because they feel that you would get hurt living the "risky" entrepreneurial life. They feel that the safer road is being in a 9 to 5 job. When you have those people in your life, you have to love them for who they are. However, you do not have to listen to what they are speaking into your life. You alone have the ability to make the best choices for your life.

Let's move on to what you are called to do. This is what brings it all together. When you know who God has called you to be, and you see yourself as how He sees you, then you are able to successfully tap into what God has called you to do. This is your #GGIF. This is the divine blend that will change your life. How do I know? I have first hand experience. I remember when I did not see myself as God sees me. He sees me as perfect. I saw myself as imperfect. I saw myself as unworthy. He sees me as worthy. God does not see me, or you, in a negative light. He sees us in His own image. That is how He made us.

When I finally realized that and got it deep down in my spirit, my whole life changed. I knew what He called me to do because it was jumping in my spirit. Every time I would have a speaking engagement, I would feel it. I would hear it knocking every time I would coach someone. God was waiting on me to do it in the natural. That way, He could put His super with my natural. Then together, we could create something supernatural. We cannot successfully tap into our #GGIF without first knowing God.

I will not assume that everyone reading this book has a personal relationship with God, so I want to take a moment to let you know that there is a prayer that you can pray to create this relationship with God. All of those who are in close connection with God said it at one point in their lives. No matter what you have done, what you are doing and what you will do in your life,

God is not mad at you. In fact, He is madly in love with you. You are the apple of His eye.

Here's a simple prayer for you to practice from www.salvationprayer.info:

● ● ● ● ● ●

Dear God in Heaven,

I come to you in the name of Jesus. I acknowledge to you that I am a sinner, and I am sorry for my sins and the life that I have lived; I need your forgiveness.

I believe that your only begotten Son, Jesus Christ, shed His precious blood on the cross at Calvary and died for my sins, and I am now willing to turn from my sin.

You said in Your Holy Word, Romans 10:9 that if we confess the Lord our God and believe in our hearts that God raised Jesus from the dead, we shall be saved. Right now, I confess Jesus as the Lord of my soul. With my heart, I believe that God raised Jesus from the dead.

> *This very moment, I accept Jesus Christ as my own personal Savior, and according to His business right now I am saved.*
>
> *Thank you, Jesus, for your unlimited grace which has saved me from my sins. I thank you, Jesus, that your grace never leads to license, but rather it always leads to repentance.*
>
> *Therefore, Lord Jesus, transform my life so that I may bring glory and honor to you alone and not to myself. Thank you, Jesus, for dying for me and giving me eternal life.*
>
> *Amen.*

Whooo! Congratulations! I am so excited for you. We have talked about how God sees you, we have talked about how you see yourself, and we have talked about your divine calling. We have given you the basic elements of your God Given It Factor.

I wanted to make sure that we created a strong foundation. It is imperative. Why? Because without it we are building on faulty land. Enjoy YOUR journey and rock your #GGIF

Stevii

2

Must Have Principle:

Spirituality

VERNA V. NICKELBERRY

So, how is it that *spirituality* fits into your *"It Factor?"* Believe it or not, your spirituality is a big part of your "It Factor." I don't mean in a religion sense, but the human side of you. It's about your soul, your inner being, and the more you listen to the voice of God, the more your spiritual *"It Factor"* will begin to come through.

Often, we ask the question, "What is my purpose here on earth?" It may seem that you are wandering around trying to figure out what to do with your life. Or you will ask yourself, "Why am I here?" At this point, I would tell you to turn to God and ask Him what it is that you would have me do.

He knows us better than anyone. In the book of Jeremiah, Chapter one, Verse five, God tells

Jeremiah *that "Before I formed thee in the belly I knew thee,"* and the same is for us as well.

As you begin to seek the will of God for your life, listen closely to His instruction. He will give you direction for every aspect of your life: ***"But seek ye first the kingdom of God, and his righteousness; and all these things shall be added unto you..."*** Matthew 6: 33. Now keep in mind that you must create space in your day-to-day activities to spend time with God. This can be 30 minutes in the morning before beginning your day or 30 minutes before going to bed. Create an oasis in a small section of your bedroom, or just a quiet place where you can go to get in the face of God. During this time, you will slowly begin to develop a personal and deep relationship with God. You may even notice small changes in yourself. Your outlook on life will begin to change as well, and that burning question, "What is my purpose here on earth?" won't seem as bleak any more.

I can remember feeling this way when I was younger, feeling very different from many of my friends and a little awkward in certain settings. This was due, in large part, because I spent a lot of time in church reading. At this time, I had no idea how much I loved going to church; I went because my mom made us go on Sundays. We would go to our church in the morning, and to other churches in the evenings. Of course, we felt that she just didn't have anything else to do and just dragged us along with her. Now as I look back it was the best thing that she could have done for us. It made me the person I am today. There is nothing like being in the face of God. Being in His presence is an awesome feeling. This is the spirituality that most seek. This is the Spirituality that gets you through the toughest and most difficult times of your life, knowing that you have developed a personal relationship with God, and that He has your back no matter what! Hebrew 13: 15 tell us: ***"Let your conversation be without covetousness; and be content with such things as ye have; for he hath said, I will never leave thee, nor forsake thee."***

As I began to mature in the word of God, I realized that I could take comfort knowing that God would always be there for me. In knowing this, it makes life a little easier. Trials and tribulations will still come, but I hold on to the word of God. You will see that God will never give you more than you can bear. He knows what our strengths are, as well as our weaknesses. And with that being said, I'm reminded of a scripture: ***"What shall we then say to these things? If God be for us, who can be against us?" – Romans 8:31***

Everything that we need is in the word of God (the Bible). I am a firm believer of divine order, meaning that even before we are born God has already put things in order for our lives. He knows what it is that we are to do. He knows why we were created and for what purpose we were created for. It is us who don't know and waste time trying to figure it out. You may find yourself asking the question, *"What is my life purpose here on earth?"* Often you may find yourself moving from one project to another and not achieving that feeling of fulfillment.

I can remember this happening to me. I was involved in so many projects, and yet I was not satiated by any of them, so I took a step back and began to evaluate my life and my purpose. I started to seek the will of God for my life more. What would He have me to do? Show me my purpose. ***"And we know that all things*** *work together for good to them that love God, to them who are the called according to his purpose." Romans 8:28*

As you begin to embark on your business journey, seek God in all of your decisions. Ask for wisdom, for guidance, and for a clear understanding of the vision that He has given, so that you will know what it is that you are to do. *"And the Lord answered me, and said Write the vision, and make it plain upon tables, that he may run that readeth it." Habakkuk 2:2*

When I read this scripture, I think of a business plan. Make sure that your business plan is clear, so that when you present it to a bank or to anyone else, it will state the exact goals of your company and how you intend to expand as you create your signature brand.

Your journey is your journey; it is uniquely yours, designed with you in mind. At times it will seem hard, but remember that God gave you the vision, and that He will be with you every step of the way. He is your counselor, your teacher, and the roadmap to your destiny. For the word of God is life, and it can surely breathe life in your business as well. *"Thy word is a lamp unto my feet, and a light unto my path." Psalm 119:105*

Stay focused, and stay on the path that God has set before you. Be careful of the counsel that you seek. "Counsel?" you may ask. I am referring to seeking the opinion of others. Remember that the counsel of God is firm. *"The counsel of the Lord standeth for ever." Psalm 33:11.*

When God gave me the assignment of producing a magazine, I didn't know where to begin. Still, I accepted the assignment, albeit reluctantly. One of the first things that I did was research the start-up cost of a magazine, which was more than I could afford. Not only that, but I didn't have anyone I could ask for help or to tell me where I should begin.

I wondered, where do I start? What do I do first? Just how do I create a magazine? I took all of my questions back to God, the giver of all visions. And so it was He who guided me from the start to the finish of the first magazine, leading me and instructing me on what to do and with whom to do it.

"Take fast hold of instruction; let her not go; keep her; for she is thy life." Proverbs

4:13 This scripture is simply saying to follow instructions and hold tight to good instruction because it is good for your life.

Although it may get tough, and it will seem as if everything is against you during your journey, hold firm, because God has got you! Don't give up, and don't give in! Be like the tree planted by the rivers of water! *"And he shall be like a tree planted by the rivers of waters, that bringeth forth his fruit in his season; his leaf also shall not wither; and whatsoever he doeth shall prosper." Psalm 1:3*

During these times, read your word more, and God will start speaking to you through his written word. Search the Bible for scriptures that will help you stay focused. Place them where you can see them, and read them throughout the day. You can even place them in your car, at your desk at your job, and on the mirror in your bathroom. Remember that the word of God is life.

You will be surprised how much this will help you, not to mention brighten up your day. This is how your spirituality will begin to grow. The more time you spend with God, allowing Him to lead you and teach you in *all things business,* you will see a big difference in your business and in the life as well. Slowly, you will step outside the box and into your creativity. Your thinking will go from what you want to do, to what God would have you do. Now you are developing a personal relationship with God, which is a good thing. This will only help you as your business grows.

Come outside of the four walls of your office and step into the world of networking and collaboration. With your newfound inner being (spirituality), you should feel comfortable in any setting. You should be able to move within in-group settings to express yourself if the occasion arises, allowing you to expand your business. You are confident, and you have the assurance that God is with you. No, this is not arrogance; it is you and God working together to get the job done in excellence. *"This also cometh forth from the Lord of hosts, which is wonderful in counsel, and excellent in working." Isaiah 28-29*

With every new project, always seek God first. Refer back to your notes from the beginning (your business plan) as you incorporate new ideas. Keep your mind sharp and fresh. Research your field of expertise often to ensure that you are always in the know and are aware of any changes.

I spend many hours watching webinars about the magazine world so I will know what to add or not add to my publication. Often, I will notice how some publications are printing the same thing that I am, but in a different manner. Many publications may be reporting on the same event, but are showing it in a different light. So continual education is very important, especially since so much education these days, like most webinars, is free.

Collaboration is one way of expanding your business and building relationships with other businesses.

Don't be afraid to partner with other business owners. This is a plus, for you and for them. You see, once you allow God to lead and guide you, things will get easier. This might not happen at first, but it will happen as you grow into the person that God has intended you to be. And we all want to be the person that God intended for us to be.

Last but not least, as your business grows and you become more confident in what you are doing, give back to your community. Your purpose in your business and in your life is not for you alone; it is for you to help others as well. There are many businesses that help non-profit organizations. This allows them to be more visible in the community and connect with those in need. Helping others will bring you so much joy and will be good for your business. Through developing your relationship with God, and following God's instructions, your business will flourish.

Most importantly, stay on the path that God has set before you, no matter what. Your obstacles are only stepping-stones to something better and greater! Stay focused, stay prayed up, and stay in the face of God! Stick with God, and you will not go wrong.

Congratulations through the word of God your "Spirituality" has been cultivated!

Verna

3

Must Have Principle:

Authentic Identity

DEBRAYTA (DEE) SALLEY

One of the most difficult and frustrating places to be in life is trying to successfully walk in your God-designed purpose and make a visible impact in the world without first taking the time to get to know who you are at your core. Your core is your innermost level of being and represents who God made you to be from the beginning of time—a designer's original.

It is the "you" that existed before you were changed by all of the hurts, the challenges, the disappointments, the frustrations, and the self-defeating habits you may have developed in your life. It is that clean slate and place of innocence from which your life's journey began to form.

You are the resilient and determined individual you are today because of your ability to bounce back and keep it moving past all those wonderful detours and obstacles. But know that neither those things nor those accomplishments clearly define the true essence of who you are. In order for your life to make the full impact that God has intended, you must first commit to the process of self- discovery and awaken your true identity. So let's get started.

What is self-discovery anyway?

According to the Merriam-Webster Dictionary, *self-discovery is defined as the act or process of gaining knowledge or understanding of your abilities, character, and feelings.* We each have a unique set of character and personality traits that, when fully activated, allows us to show up in the world as different reflections of who we are, each of us special in the sight of God. The Father purposely made each of us unique, and as a result, no matter how hard we may try, we will not be able to change that. As a matter of fact, no one else will be able to successfully duplicate you either. He doesn't want to use some of you, but rather all of you, so He can fulfill His purpose in the earth.

In Jeremiah 1:5, He told us this Himself: *"Before I formed you in the womb, I knew you. Before you were born, I set you apart for my holy purpose."* Not only that, but He shows us just how serious He is about our unique characteristics by being able to account for the number of hairs on our head.

In Luke 12:7, He proudly informs us that *"Indeed, the very hairs of your head are all numbered. Don't be afraid; you are worth more than many sparrows."* Now, I would have to say that you are some kind of special! Don't you agree? As you nod your head YES, I want you to keep these facts at the forefront of your mind and as the foundation of how you see yourself from this point forward because as you move through your journey, your confidence and faith in them will be tested.

For example, we live in a world where differences are not always celebrated, and if you are not careful, you may be tempted to try to "fit-in" rather than "standout." I want to encourage you to resist the urge to do this at all costs! The quickest way to abort your personal brand or identity is to dress it up to look like someone else's, or to tweak it so that your differences won't scream out, "Look at me, I'm different!" On the contrary, that's exactly what you have to do if you are going to be all that God has destined you to be so you can impact those whom you are meant to serve. God wants you to embrace all of who you are—the things you see as flaws, the things that make you stick out like a "sore thumb," and the things that make you downright uncomfortable.

Typically, the character or personality traits that we deem as useless are the very things that God wants to use to grow and prosper us. Now, understand this, once you begin to appreciate and begin to awaken all the pieces of who you are, you will feel like a "fish out of water" for a while, but once you get the hang of it and make it your rule of thumb, you will become a professional at being your authentic self. As we move forward, I'd like to point out that it is extremely important to be aware of the fact that your journey of self-discovery is not a one-time occurrence.

You will not necessarily wake up the morning after reading this and be all that you will ever be in this lifetime. In comparison to any other phase of your life's journey, this will be a process that you get to enjoy for the rest of your years, starting now. My assignment here is to help you see that the process is much more exciting and devoid of stress when you willingly submit to the idea and fully understand that we didn't come here as a package marked with specific "handling instructions."

Now, after you have accepted who you are in Christ, embraced your uniqueness, and submitted to the journey of self- discovery, you may at times be in situations and circles where you are tempted to conform or adapt like a chameleon to your surroundings. There will be times when you are aware that this is transpiring; however, there will be many other occasions when it will happen without you even realizing it unless you have committed to the discovery process.

For example, have you ever witnessed an introverted or quiet person attempt to be the life of the party? You may have observed that not only did that person look uncomfortable, but those around them either didn't notice, or were enjoying a good laugh at his expense. Then, what about the extroverted person who is always the life of the party, but one day she is found sitting alone away from the crowd, seemingly uncomfortable? In that instance, you may have thought that they must be either sad because of something that happened or an illness. Imagine how awkward and stressful it would be for a person to internally ignore their feelings and disguise their individuality solely to avoid criticism or ridicule from others.

Also, let's not forget about the disappointment that God must feel when we reject his proud masterpiece. I liken this to a child being so ashamed of his/her parents and the life he has that he never allows his friends to meet them or ever talk about their home life. Well, you get the point that I am trying to make: We have been granted this one chance at life to live it to the fullest, and it would be hard to do that if we suppress who we truly are. Don't ever dim your light, because you are a star in a huge galaxy of individual stars that all make the night sky a beautiful sight! *Amen.*

I am keenly aware that not everyone reading this is at the same place in his or her life's journey or level of personal development, so I hope that you can take away the nuggets that suit you personally. There are, without a doubt, some who may be reading this that have made personal development and self-discovery a part of their individual lifestyles. To those individuals, I'd like to ask, have you ever thought that you had yourself all figured out and knew all there was to know about you, and then BOOM! God provided a situation or a revelation that made you see that there was more to be awakened? I'm laughing out loud right now because for me personally, this became a regular occurrence, as I would get a piece of the puzzle and take off running to carry it out. I've learned that doing that is like watching the first five minutes of a movie and then turning it off and assuming you know how it is going to end. Sometimes, while we may be excited about the preview of coming attractions, we have to sit ourselves down and wait for the full report. *Amen.*

Here is a snapshot of my personal journey:

I began my entrepreneurial journey many years ago as a representative for a candle company sharing beautiful scents along with encouraging personal messages with my orders, and almost six years later, I'm an author who has accepted my divine assignment to share hope, encouragement, and resources by way of writing and speaking so I can assist those who have been broken by life challenges or are in the midst of a life transition. To be blunt, I spent many years roaming endlessly, attending workshops and events, reading books, etc. in search of the real me, but I was never truly successful until I intentionally sought out to know my Heavenly Father and examine how he had wired me as an individual. I was looking for the real me all over and there it was all of the time, my reflection, in the mirror right smack in front of me. I just needed to get up close and personal with the real me. Now, please don't get me wrong, I wouldn't trade anything for my journey because I know that it served a higher purpose, but I'm sure that I could have knocked a few years off of the process had I taken the steps needed to awaken my true identity earlier on.

So how will you know when you have begun to awaken your true identity? Here are just a few examples:

- When you no longer see the things that make you different as "flaws," but instead see them as strengths that set you apart as an individual.

- When you no longer desire to be anyone but the person that God has ordained and designed you to be.

- When you stop making excuses and stop apologizing for who you are, and can just BE.

- When you no longer suppress your true feelings and desires just so you can be in the company of others.

- When you become humble and naked before God and ask him to show you who you are and what purpose you are meant to serve.

- When you no longer dim your light to fit in, but instead let it shine brightly like the diamond you are.

- When you realize that you can be bold and happy standing out from the crowd because you are a brilliant star in a beautiful sky full of individual stars that each serves a purpose.

- When you can show up as the same person, whether it be in a board meeting, a social gathering, or a meeting with a client, because the essence of the person you are has been released and follows you wherever you go.

- When your relationships are no longer unfruitful because they are based on someone you portray yourself to be. Instead, they are fruitful because you are secure with your authentic self and only allow others into your space who respect the real you.

In closing, the more of the authentic YOU that is released into the earth, the more you will experience an uninhibited force of authenticity in your interactions and allow God to show up in every facet of your life to carry out His plans for you.

If you are still reading this, I believe that you are about to either embark on a life changing journey of self-discovery or that God is about to show you that there is more to you than you thought existed.

I challenge you to be bold and intentional as your true identity is awakened!

Enjoy the process. Enjoy the journey!

Dee

4

Must Have Principle:

Soul Nourishment

M.E. PORTER

et's take a long walk, around the park, after dark, yeah. Find a spot for us to spark conversation, verbal elation, stimulation. Share our situations, temptations, education, relaxations. Elevations, maybe we can talk about Surah 31," sang Jilly from Philly! I love my Saturday morning playlist: a little Indie, some Maxwell, and a tad bit of Brian McKnight in the mix—ALWAYS!

Music soothes my soul; it calms me, centers me and prepares me for whatever will come next. Music is like prayer to me. Something about the vibrations of the instruments and voices reaches to my core. So every Saturday morning, especially on my "SaturME" – Saturdays (which are every 3rd one of every month), as soon as I rise, the computer comes on, the playlist is pulled up, and I begin to deal with the matters of my soul: healing, freeing, soothing, and nourishment.

I spent many years of my life with a true misunderstanding of what it meant to be a servant leader. As a child, I watched my mom and other women around me literally run themselves into the ground. Taking care of children—often alone—working full-time jobs and serving on the church usher board, all while catering to husbands and boyfriends effectively (or it seemed to be effectively from my child state of mind). They made it all seem so easy and possible to be the servant to all, while proudly announcing to anyone who would listen that they had not had a good night's sleep in years, or had no time to sit still long enough to digest a good meal or enough money to even purchase themselves a pair of new panties. WOW! These were the strongest women in the world, and I wanted to grow up and be just as "super-womanish" as they all were.

I was around 13 years old when my mom first called me into her bedroom to beat her in the back. She would have these horrible bouts of indigestion that would land her in the emergency room if my back pounding (which was, in essence, me trying to burp her the way you burp a newborn baby) did not work. My mom was 33 years old and already had a diagnosed ulcerated stomach (a condition that had been fatal to her mother), hypertension, fibroids, and migraines. This was when I began to get a clear understanding that being a servant to others does not mean that you have to do a disservice to yourself. So there I sat, in an ER with mother, who, at 33 years old was so ill in her body that she needed a medical team for simple food digestion. What was even more awakening were the words I heard the doctor declare: "Miss Porter, many of the ailments you have are stress induced! You are going to have to commit to finding some form of stress-relief or these problems will persist." So I decided that day that the superwoman thing might not be —nah, certainly was not— for me.

Mom found her path to stress relief in the forms of Bingo and Tunk, but her newfound hobbies left me to care for my younger siblings...*bummer*. I came to know those same sleepless nights that I had often heard my mother and the other superwomen in my neighborhood speak of. My little brother was super active. I swear, that boy would never go to sleep! But because I didn't want my mom stressed (sick), I learned to maintain straight A's in school, care for my two siblings, and be a reliable daughter, a loyal friend, and all around go-to girl.

At age 15, I began to feel sick. I had headaches, toothaches (my mouth is my stress point, so when any other part of my body is stressed my mouth hurts too), muscle aches, and a loss of appetite. Plus, I was becoming a little bit mean to my siblings. I WAS STRESSED! At 15, I didn't have a lot of options to relieve my stress, but I did have God and music. These became my places of refuge, my solace, and my soul retreat; I felt God in the music and it gave me relief.

I have since become much more aware of the awesomeness of life and all that it can offer to us and our senses. I find freshness for my soul in many things, but God and prayer have become my primary resources. Music, romance, and friendship run a very close second. Good food, bright colors, a fabulous hairstyle, and the funkiest stiletto or baaaaaaaad handbag—I am a designer handbag girl for sure! Coach™

is soothing to my soul! Although it may seem as though I am making light of such a serious matter, trust me, I have an appreciation for beautiful things that my heart can feel, my eyes can see, my ears can hear, my heart can love, my hands can touch. I am nourished by the blessings of my living environment, my senses. If you will, I'd like to offer you a bit of a roadmap to experience life as I do. Let's tend to the matters of the soul.

What is this *soul* I speak of, and why does it need to be tended to? Good questions. The soul is the absolute essence of YOU. It is the purest place of your existence. In fact, I believe this is where God resides in us. This is the truest, most authentic, most recognizable version of you. Even in another person's body, YOUR soul would show up as YOU. The mind can be altered. Emotions change as often and as easy as the wind blows. The spirit will sing when it really wants to cry, but the soul remains true to your exact state of being. The body can be trained to do that which we desire, but the soul remains true to the divine design, and it aches when it is left uncared for. The soul comes with an assignment to carry out, and it will not adjust to situations and circumstances.

Thus, when left beaten, battered, and bruised, the soul must struggle to complete its assignment in a broken state. This is why soul food is necessary. The great success of Jack Canfield's book series, "Chicken Soup for The Soul," is primarily based on this fact: We must tend to the matters of the soul.

And now, the why. Even if you have never been on an airplane, I am sure that you've heard the statement "put the oxygen on yourself first," which simply translates to "save yourself first so that you are able to save another." The most effective way to serve others is to first care for YOU, the real you, the you that can reach out and touch another person's life without even speaking a word and still make your mere presence life changing. Have you ever heard of someone being spoken of in these terms: "There is just something about him. When he walks into the room, the atmosphere changes"? Those are the people who tend to matters of the soul. They, like myself, find nourishment in the beauty of the environment and creation, who indulge the senses in beauty of a holy creation—love, food, music, poetry, art, gardening, and yes a funky stiletto and a sharp Coach™ bag.

Rest, relaxation, prayer meditation, long walks, short talks, a perfect cup of coffee, or a slice of cake with just the right amount of sweetness. A fine, clean-shaven man, the smell of a new car, the crease in the collar of your favorite suit or the messy, smelly, germy mud pie plopped in your face by an excited five-year old. Why does the soul require care? Because you need to thrive at this thing called life. YOU must LIVE!

I am a minister of the Gospel. I am a mother. I am a business woman, a CEO. I am a thought leader. I am a friend. I am a lover. I am an intellect. I am a survivor. I am a woman. I am often operating several roles simultaneously. My thoughts become jumbled, my emotions get rattled, and my body gets tired, but when my soul is nourished, all is well in the world.

In the seat of chaos and the constant flow of negative chatter around me, when my soul is nourished, all is well in the world. When I am up against a deadline and I have more money due than money earned, if my soul is nourished, all is well in the world. When my kindness has been taken for weakness and my trust has been betrayed, if my soul is nourished, all is well in the world. When my children don't appreciate my sacrifice and my love does not console, my surface hurts; if my soul is nourished, all is well in the world. With no pat on the back, no "thank you," no "I am sorry," no "everything will be okay," if my soul is nourished, all is well with the world. The music begins to play. The savory smell of my favorite meal graces my nostrils. I feel the gentle wind on my skin or the sun on my face.

I walk past my closet and see a bright pink dress hanging there and a smile emerges on my face that flutters my soul—color, yes my friend color, nourishes my soul. Or I catch a glimpse of my image in the mirror, and I trust that God's design is marvelously perfect; this earthly suit that houses ME is fabulous.

I love living this soul-filled life! Allow me to offer you some insight to my soul-care techniques:

- Love every good and perfect thing, including you. Embrace the totality of you. Yes, we all have things that need improvement, but know that improvement does not come as harsh judgment; it comes with learning to love who you are, where you are, while you are there.

- Prayer is a must. Prayer is a glorious opportunity to commune with creation and the Creator. Prayer is not a monologue; it is a dialogue, so sit and listen. Don't just speak and move on to the next task of the day.

- Believe that every moment of your life is exactly as it should be. Trust that the core of who you are is always prepared and equipped to respond to the current circumstance. NO mistakes. NO wrong turns. NO coincidences. All is well at all times.

- Receive the grace that is given to you to BE YOU. We each have the grace to function as our soul-selves with ease. The struggle comes from going against who you really are. When you wake in the morning, be thankful for the grace that hovers over your life, allowing you to permit yourself to simply and easily be you.

- Give yourself the gift of saying "yes" when the answer should be yes, and "NO" when the answer should be no. Both are complete sentences that don't require explanations. Give others the freedom to be who they are designed to be. Don't infringe your make and model onto others. This is a surefire way to disturb your own soul-rest. Although ego may be flattered with a carbon copy of you walking around, your soul does not desire to be duplicated, because its job is to be the essence of YOU and no one else.

- Forgive yourself and others for the mistakes that are built into your path. Remember, nothing is an accident or coincidence. All is as it should be at all times. Appreciate all aspects of the journey. This means forgiveness, which means you are moving beyond the infraction. It doesn't require you to continue on in a relationship, or be connected to the person, but you must move beyond hating, despising, blaming, and plotting against others. The soul cries when weighed down by a lack of forgiveness and its crippling effects.

- Nourishment is food, care, cultivating, pampering, truth telling, regular assessments, and all things affectionate and loving.

"Love, exciting and new come aboard. We're expecting you. And Love, life's sweetest reward. Let it flow, it floats back to you. Love Boat soon will be making another run. The Love Boat promises something for everyone. Set a course for adventure, Your mind on a new romance. And Love won't hurt anymore It's an open smile on a friendly shore.

Yes LOOOOOOOOOOOOOOOVE!

Welcome Aboard.

It's LOOOOOOOOOOOOOOOVE!"

As I prepare to lay my head down on my pillow at night—yes, even this very night—my soul is smiling because I allow it the freedom to love what it loves and it loves "The Love Boat." Don't judge me, join me. What thing makes your soul smile that you have been depriving it of? What seemingly corny, unconventional, uncool, un-adult thing makes your soul smile? My dear friend, find the things that soothe your soul.

Dealing with matters of the soul is a must. It will not be denied and you will not feel whole until the soul is nourished.

Matters of the soul are the matters of life, and YOU must live!

M.E.

5

Must Have Principle:

Courage

FUNGAI NDEMERA

Since I was a little girl, I dreamt of being my own boss. While other young girls pretended to be the perfect bride or fantasized about their dream home, I was coming up with creative ways to make my own money. Born into a small, poverty-stricken, rural area in Mhondoro, Zimbabwe, I learned the value of money at a very young age.

Growing up, my mom could not afford to give me much money, and because of this, I valued every opportunity that came my way to earn my own income. My uncle would give me "pocket change" whenever he came into town, and this money was supposed to buy my necessities for that day. Now, most children would run to the nearest store and spend all of their money on snacks and candies to eat. Not me.

I didn't mind going without my snacks for the day. I began saving my pocket change and any other money given to me, and I began on my journey of entrepreneurship. I took this money that I had saved and used it to buy packs of what we called chip sticks, and then I would resell them.

This business took off, and before I knew it I would sell out within a day. This became my little business at school and in my neighborhood. I made a whopping 86 cents off of each sale. Now that may not seem like a lot to you, but 30 years ago—especially for an 8-year-old—that was a lot of money! This was my "lemonade stand." My bank account was a tin can that sat in a small hole in the back of my house, covered with soil. No one ever knew it was there. I'd pull out just enough to purchase my products and save the rest. And this was my very first experience of entrepreneurship.

Today, I'm grateful to say that I run a seven-figure business that I built from scratch, and I have the honor of helping women that know they want to make a difference, and lead rich, meaningful, and abundant lives through entrepreneurship.

My clients are compassionate, committed, and driven to create income that is true to their highest intention.

I often look back at that moment in my life when I made the decision to be my own boss. That moment was a pivotal point in which I knew I was destined to serve a higher calling. The road to success hasn't been laced with gold or easy, by far. In fact, the fear of showing up in the world legitimately sabotaged my business and brand before it even successfully left the ground. I was afraid of failing, as many of you can relate to. But failing is all a part of the process.

In failing, I found many ways not to run my business, and I found new and amazing ways to grow my brand. It wasn't until I realized that I am the author of my own life, just like you are the author of yours. If you don't like something about your story, you have the right to change it. You can write yourself a new story, much like I did. I learned to move beyond the harsh realities of my society and create the life I loved. You, too, can write the life you want to lead.

It took a lot of hard work, dedication, and consistency to build a seven-figure powerhouse brand. And today, I am going to teach you how to do the same thing. Frequently, my inbox floods with questions from potential clients wanting to know how to get started with their brand, how to define their message, or how to create the perfect strategy for running their businesses. Because of this, I have pulled five of the top questions I am asked on a daily basis, and I want to answer them right here for you. I recommend grabbing a pen and paper, and getting yourself ready to build your signature brand.

Let's get started.

Where Should I Start With Building My Signature Brand?

In order to build a signature brand, it's important to analyze what holds you back and to start moving away from those unhealthy, sabotaging habits. When I first started my business, the thing that held me back the most was fear. Can you relate? Fear was the boss of me. But the truth is we all experience fear in some form or another, especially as entrepreneurs. We are often in a state of navigating unknown territory, and always trying to find our way. Most experiences are unpredictable, and this leaves us terrified to push forward and follow our dreams. But before we move forward, let's get rid of the big elephant in the room.

Let's address the fear of failing, shall we? You want to start your new business. You want to live that dream life that you've imagined for yourself and your family. You've dreamt of how your products and services will change the world, but you think you're not good enough to be successful. No one will want your products. No one will purchase your services. You tell yourself that you'll be laughed at, and you'll never hit your goals. Does any of this sound familiar? I know these thoughts all too well. How? Because they used to be mine.

Here's the thing: I failed all the time. In fact, I still do! The key to failing is learning from your failure. Each time I fail at one thing, I take it, analyze it, and use it to develop my skillset and myself so my business can grow into an even better signature brand. Because, in actuality, failing isn't failing at all. You just learn a different, more effective way to nurture your brand.

So what about you? How is fear holding you back from building your signature brand? Take some time to list your fears right now. This may be challenging, but the first step is to acknowledge them. Next to each fear, write down a solution to eliminate it. For example, if your fear is recording videos of yourself, your solution can be to record your first video and upload it to your website or social media channel by the end of the week. After you have listed all your fears and solutions, choose ONE that you can focus on today to get you moving beyond your fear and into building your signature brand.

How Do I Use My Story To Build My Signature Brand?

Learning to use your story to build your brand is critical for your success. It allows you to take a brave look at yourself and give yourself a big dose of self-awareness before launching your beautiful brand and story into the world. Many of the most resonating signature brands are driven by their stories. Think about a brand that resonates with you the most. For me, it's Oprah. Her story of poverty, struggle, and success is part of her signature brand. It's what moves her listeners, readers, and followers. It's that part of her brand that's vulnerable and gives us all an opportunity to say "me too."

When you confront your story, something beautiful happens. You learn to move THROUGH your fear. You acknowledge that telling your story is scary and uncomfortable, but you know it serves a higher power. And you do it. And you're okay. You create a safe space where the magnitude of who you truly are can come rushing in, and you own the story that you know will change the world.

You may be thinking, "but I don't really have a story, or I have no idea where to even begin." That's just your fear talking. We all have a story. So here's your challenge: take a moment and think about where you are in life right now and how you got there. Think about that moment you triumphed in life, that moment in which you defied the odds and defeated the trials. How did that moment transform you into who you are today? How does that moment encourage you to stand tall in your power, and help others around you live a better life? Use this time to dig deep into your story and use it to attract your dream clients that will pay for your products and services over and over again.

So, What Exactly Is a Brand?

This is by far one of my favorite questions to answer. When you're first starting out, you may not know the importance of building a brand from day one. I enjoy teaching entrepreneurs all about building a signature brand, and I start by helping them understand what a brand is in the first place. So, here it goes. In short, a brand is your identity in the marketplace and your promise to deliver consistently without fail. It's how you tell your customers what they can expect from you, your products, and your services. Your brand sets you apart from your competitors.

Think about your favorite brand. Ok, you got it? Now I want you to think about what sets it apart from its competitors. What do you know them for? Your brand is how people recognize you and what they will know you for. Defining your brand can be frustrating and challenging, and it may take some time to accomplish, but in the end, it will be worth it. Here are a few #powerhousetips to help you create your powerful brand.

First, define your brand. What is it that you want people to feel when they come in contact with your brand? What is your ultimate goal with your business? Do you want people to feel empowered, educated, relieved? Do you want them to feel as if they will never need another product because yours is the ONLY ONE that they've been searching for? Take some time, and think about this question. You need to lay down the foundation of your brand. This becomes the foundation of your profitable business. If you don't have a solid foundation, you won't have anything to build on.

Next, determine what makes you different from your competitors. There will likely be tons of people in your desired niche, but what makes you stand out? Is it your authentic personality? Is it your amazing customer service? I'd challenge you to compare a few of your potential competitors. Look at what you absolutely love about their brand, and what you would do differently. How can you stand out in such a way that your dream clients will bypass your competitors without giving them a second look? Once you answer these questions, create a document and title it MY BRAND, and write down everything that your brand encompasses. This will begin your journey of building your signature brand.

How Do I Describe What I Do?

Now this is the million-dollar question, right? It very well could be a million-dollar question, depending on how you answer it. I believe strongly in building a network, and letting others know what you do. But as you know, sometimes it's not so easy to spit out all of your gifts and passion into a three-sentence spill. So what happens when you are out at the networking event, or you're in the elevator and someone asks, "What is it that you do?" The last thing you want to do is answer with a ton of "ums" and "wells."

Use this #powerhousetip to explain what you do in such a way that connects and compels with your audience.

Follow the steps on the next page.

My Name Is

_____

I Am The CEO & Founder of

_____

And I Help *(who do you help)*

_____

What do you help them do?

_____

Your finished product may look something like this:

> *My name is Fungai, I am the CEO & Founder of FungaiNdemera.com, and I help women who know they want to make a difference and lead rich, meaningful, and abundant lives through their businesses.*

Simple, right? Take some time to complete this exercise and try practicing it a few times in the mirror until you get comfortable with it.

You'll be ready in no time to explain what you do, without sounding like you haven't a clue.

How Do I Connect With My Dream Client?

Here's the thing: Let's say you create this amazing product, and you build this signature brand. And then, it sits there. And sits there. And sits there some more, collecting dust. This is not how to get to the seven-figure income you dream of. This is not how you build your signature brand. You have to BE your dream client. And for many of you who are building your business from your story, you may have been your dream client at one point of your journey.

I remember building my business and being so afraid to shine bright in the world. I was playing small. And when I started playing big, and owning my fears instead of letting my fears defeat me, I knew exactly how to help my dream client through that phase of her journey.

Here's your challenge: Take some time to write out your dream client's story, and really try to figure out her frustrations. Aim to be her solution.

What does she need?

How can you help?

Don't sell her. Use your story to connect with her.

You have a gift. There's no denying that. You wouldn't be reading this book if you didn't believe you were designed to do more, to be more. And the great thing is that you don't have to know everything to get started. You don't have to be the most brilliant or the most accomplished. You just have to get started.

I believe that we are sparked by purpose. That means that what we are truly passionate about is what we have a divine duty, or purpose, to carry out. You have all that you need to make your dreams come true, and that's the will to make it happen. If you have your heart set on growing your business, you are already one step closer to living your abundant life.

Don't let fear continue to stop you from living your bold, beautiful life. Fear is normal. I get it. I still experience fear often in my life and business. Instead of letting your fear halt your success, use your fear to grow your success. What you are most afraid of is likely what you should focus on today.

In order to build a signature brand, you must step outside of your comfort zone. You must start now. You may not feel like you're ready, but the greatest clarity comes from taking action.

When I took my first step of booking a one-way ticket from Zimbabwe to the United Kingdom, I didn't quite feel ready, but I knew in my heart that taking the first leap of faith was the right thing for me. And seven figures and hundreds of happy successful clients later, I know it was worth it.

Fungai

6

Must Have Principle:

Tenacity

RHONDA McALISTER

It took me many, many years of my life to get to the point where I was not concerned, or at least less concerned, about what people thought of me. Why is it that we are fearful of ourselves? Could it be that we are so fearful of the success that we may achieve? Most of us became fearful of ourselves because it was branded into us.

We are surrounded with individuals who think on a level smaller than, or people who do not have the same confidence in us as we may require of ourselves.

If you do not allow yourself to come out of this whirlwind of a downward spiral of your conscious thinking, then you will start to believe in small thinking patterns. For me it started with my mom.

Because I was a teen mom, I felt pressured for many years to be more than what others expected of me. My grandmother and my natural mother were both teen moms without high school diplomas. I became pregnant at 14, and I had my first child at the age of 15. I delivered my second child at the ripe old age of 16. These facts are part of my story, just like many others. Nothing really special about them, except maybe my struggles. Everyone's struggles aren't quite the same. However, it is usually not the struggle that matters, but how you come out of it.

Whether you come out on the bottom or on the top. It's about the choice or choices that you decide to make while on your journey. It's about the people you left behind so you could move on. Being a teen mom, I felt like I was a failure, because I had started my family at such a young age. Because of this, I set a goal for myself: Even though I had gotten pregnant twice in high school, and technically could have been almost two years behind, I would do whatever it took to graduate on time with my graduating class.

To accomplish this hefty goal, I went to summer school for two summers in a row, and

I had to take one class during my senior year, but I did graduate with my class and walked across the stage in 1989.

If you recall, I said it took me many years to realize this. I wonder how many of you are still trying to live your life or make your decisions based on what other people think of you. Let me assure you that no matter what you do, and no matter how well you do something, you will not be able to please everybody. There will always be someone who is not happy with the outcome—whatever it is you've done—and there will always be someone who is not happy with the decision you have made. Your mistakes will be highlighted, and your successes will be minimized. But this is life. It took me YEARS to get to the place where it no longer mattered to me. I finally realized that if I was going to make my dreams come true, it was going to be up to me and while I was waiting on someone to give me an "okay," time was passing me by. We all know the old quote that says "Time Waits for No One"; trust me, it is true.

The moment you realized God was real for you and all those prayers from your aunt, grandma, or whomever you learned to pray for yourself so you could make it, whatever YOUR "it" is. That's just a part of my story.

Now I am standing in the shoes God put on my feet to share my story to help redirect someone else. To empower someone's daughter, granddaughter, mother. Not being recognized for all of your gifts and talents is also part of running a business, but you must continue to do what is best for your progress and your success in spite of what other people may think of you.

Of course, this means, sometimes, that you may be left alone. Or you may just feel like you're standing alone. For this reason, it is important to have a support system. They may not be who you think they are. Your support system should be the same people or person who shares your business goals. If their vision does not match your vision, they should not be part of your team.

Team. Let's talk for a moment about building your team. It is true that in order to continue growing your mindset, and in order to achieve your goals, you must surround yourself with like-minded people, or even better, with people who know much more than you do. Doing this will push you to achieve your goals faster and more effectively than you ever would have done without the right TEAM in place. Everyone does not complete this seamlessly. It is important to remember that you want the members of your team to be BETTER than you and perhaps more experienced than you. Why? Because it brings better value to what you are putting together.

Remember, if you are the sharpest person on the team, REBUILD. It's great to be the best at what you do, but you cannot be the best at everything. Make room for other experts to fill the vacant positions on your team.

Make sure that your team knows their responsibilities and what areas they are supposed to manage. You need these things to be clearly outlined so that your team can function smoothly.

Many of us struggle to grow because we are concerned about what someone else will think, or what she will say about our idea, our business, or our partnerships.

Cultivating Your IT Factor

A while ago, I had the privilege of holding a workshop for some very spirited young ladies. I was once exactly like them as a teen mom. After the workshop, many of them told me how much they appreciated my time and the bits of knowledge I shared with them. That, for me, was a conformation that I was where I was supposed to be at that time.

About a year or so ago, I was really looking for something to help me find my "place." It is amazing when you know you are "out of position." God will not let you rest if He has called you to do something and you have not responded. I already knew I was to have "talks" with teen moms, and that my story was meant to change someone's life one day. And yet I hesitated and hesitated. And although my nose is exactly where it's supposed to be, I was not. I finally held the first workshop, and I have since developed my business, *Rhonda Davis Workshops*, where I have incorporated all of my workshops: *Confession of a Welfare Mom*, *Success Principles*, *The High School Entrepreneurship Program*, and *Believe to Achieve*.

I introduced what I call the S.H.I.F.T. method, which is easy for my audience to remember and to apply to their lives.

Quickly write down **five things you want to change**. It could be anything. You can mix it up with business or personal things, whatever you prefer. As I explain the process, please take notes and apply them to where it applies on your list.

Let's talk about **S.H.I.F.T.** It is an acronym that I have created to put things in order for those with a business or a service they provide to others.

• • • S is for creating <u>systems</u>.

It is important to create systems so things are still happening whether you are doing them or not, whether you are present or not. You have to systematically begin to establish this so you can set your business apart from the competition.

Take vendors, for example. If you are a vendor and you have an event, you should have an item on your table that draws customers to you. If you sell to kids, use candy or toys. If you want to appeal to women, institute a drawing for something FREE. Once they are there, you have the opportunity to engage with them. Do not sit and look at them, and do not talk to someone on your telephone; engage your customers. Encourage them to sign up for your drawing, which gives you their NAME AND EMAIL ADDRESS, minimum. Now that they are there, they can see what you have to offer. Now that they have signed up for your drawing and you have their information (let them know they'll be added to your list), you have the opportunity to not only note what they are purchasing; you can add them to your email campaign. Adding them to your campaign lets them stay informed with your new products when they come out; you can also notify them when something is going on sale and when you will be at your next event. Now that is a system.

• • • H is to **hone** in on your gifts, qualities, and talents. This is where you monetize what you already love to do. This adds revenue to your business or service. Three ways to add revenue to your business are: speaking, writing, and creating products.

• • • I is **investing** in you. You will have to take a class, find a mentor, and hire a coach in order to continue to learn and be successful. Learning is forever. It never ends. If you are not willing to invest in your future, neither will anyone else. You'd be surprised who's watching you to see if you are sincere about your business or service.

• • • F means that **failure** is not an option. People fail from a lack of knowledge, a lack of capital, and a lack of resources.

• • • T is for **time management**. When you are starting your business or service, "time management" will seem impossible, which is why creating systems is very important. If you're actually building a company or an enterprise, you will, over time, develop a TEAM and be able to delegate tasks so you don't have to do everything from budgets to planning lunches. In the meantime, you have to learn how to use services such as *Fiverr* and *Mailchimp* to outsource some of your tasks.

Another useful tip is to put every task on your calendar. Whether it's appointments for the kids, meetings, or calls that need to be made, put in on there. This way nothing gets overlooked, and you can cover all of your bases. Once you are doing this, it will be easy to begin your day by looking at your calendar first thing in the morning and scheduling your day appropriately to ensure that it runs smoothly.

If you have an extremely hectic schedule or are perhaps traveling often, I suggest scheduling your time in small increments, like 15 minutes, and setting reminders on your cellphone to keep you on task.

You now have the information you need to begin thinking about where your journey needs to begin. You now understand that it is okay to stand on your own if you are required to do so. You now recognize that you have to create your own belief system and build your support team of peers and experts in order to be successful. But the most important concept that you must realize is this: We are not the people of our past; we are not the people that someone used to know.

Do not be caught up in the whirlwind of believing that you are not worthy of your own success. Your success story will not be like someone else's, so there's no need to try to mimic someone else's success. Once you stop believing what other people believe about you, and instead start growing yourself and start introducing yourself to new mindsets, new strategies, and new networking partnerships, then you will have the power to eliminate the fear of believing in yourself and start understanding that you are worth the success for which you were aiming.

Rhonda

7

Must Have Principle:

Value Awareness

CYNETA HILL

When you choose to become an entrepreneur, it is vital to understand your value in order to build your wealth. Value is needed to make smart decisions and moves as an entrepreneur. Value allows you as an entrepreneur to take risks and accept new opportunities as you build wealth. I would like to say that again.

It is very important to **understand your value in order to build your wealth**! In this particular chapter, we will discuss the principles of value, value struggles, value building, steps to create wealth, and strategies for expanding value to increase wealth.

Throughout the chapter, I will challenge you to participate in personal value-building exercises.

Get ready to put on your running shoes as we run the golden road of identifying value based strategies and solutions to build wealth.

In order to better understand your **value,** let's examine its definition. Webster defines value as the amount of money that something is worth and the price or cost of something. Webster also defines value as "usefulness" or "importance." My definition of value is righteously making a positive change in the world by providing treasured services or products so I can meet individuals' day-to-day needs and provide them with the means necessary of building a quality of life while also building wealth. It is very important to have a clear understanding of value in order to bring forth the full effect of what God has destined you to do.

In understanding value, you must be aware of the following contributing practice principles: moral values and ethics.

Moral values may be defined as your behavior model of conduct that is deemed most worthwhile by society. A moral value is an action that fosters human well being, unity, and cohesiveness in human relationships.

A habit of good moral value develops conduct that is considered good in order to promote human and social welfare.

- What personal moral value do you personally implement on a daily basis? How can it contribute to building your wealth?

For example, I value helping people fulfill their personal and professional goals. As a result of my moral value, I provide small group goal-building sessions in order to build wealth.

Your turn:

I value helping people fulfill

_____

As a result of my moral value, I...

_____

_____

_____

_____

"Your value is your key source to success"
– C. Hill

One could ask, how do values relate to ethics, and what exactly are "ethics?" Ethics is a set of principles and practices we view as a right or wrong, and a standard is set to determine how we implement those practices.

When seeking entrepreneurship, exercising sound ethics values can be challenging for some to adhere to as an entrepreneur due to the urgent need to gain wealth. However, doing what is right increases positive attributes to both society and yourself. To act ethically is to act in a way that is consistent with what is right or moral. I am a firm believer in honoring and valuing God in everything I do. Therefore, I base my four personal and professional codes of ethics in His word, and I hope it is beneficial to you.

My Personal Value Ethics

- **Honesty**: Finally, brothers, whatever is true, whatever is honorable, whatever is just, whatever is pure, whatever is lovely, whatever is commendable, if there is any excellence, if there is anything worthy of praise, think about these things. What you have learned and received and heard and seen in me—practice these things, and the God of peace will be with you. (Phil 4:8-9)

- **Trust**: Trust in the Lord with all your heart, and do not lean on your own understanding. In all your ways acknowledge him, and he will make straight your paths. Be not wise in your own eyes; fear the Lord, and turn away from evil. It will be healing to your flesh and refreshment to your bones. Honor the Lord with your wealth and with the first fruits of all your produce (Proverbs 3:5-12)

- **Respect**: So whatever you wish that others would do to you, do also to them, for this is the Law and the Prophets. (Matt 7:12)

- **Authenticity**: For we hear that some among you walk in idleness, not busy at work, but busybodies. Now such persons we command and encourage in the Lord Jesus Christ to do their work quietly and to earn their own living. (2 Thessalonians 3: 11-12)

The beautiful thing about basing my personal and professional code of ethics on the word of God is that it leads to wealth in God's eyes, which is the value I honor the most. Being honest in everything you do brings peace, develops trust, and keeps you on a straight path, since you treat others as you want to be treated. Showing others the authentic value of respect provides a sense of self-worth and wealth. I hope you see where I am going with this. Wealth does not have to be built on worldly expectations. In fact, you can create it yourself the right way, and you'll find that doing so will be much more rewarding.

Many people do not realize how important their value is, which leads to complacency, excuses, laziness, and stunted personal and professional growth. Once you realize your true value, your entire thought and action-process changes. Now that we know the meaning of value, I want you to take the time to complete your personal value pledge.

This pledge will help you to appreciate your value when you face struggles as you build worthy wealth:

I, _____, am a value change agent.

I value the ability to have life more abundantly.

My abundant living will be based on these ethics:

_____, _____, & _____.

My value ethics will keep me grounded as I implement the following values:

_____, _____, & _____.
as I build wealth in God.

Although there is sometimes success in having values, as a result of these same values, you will face struggles. Value struggles as an entrepreneur can be hard to cope with when your net profits start to decrease. Anyone knows that struggling isn't fun personally or professionally.

However, as a result of having righteous values, you sometimes have to walk away or disconnect yourself from people, places, jobs, and organizations that are not aligned with your values so you can do what you know is right.

I personally know firsthand how this feels because I walked away from a job that placed value on profit versus providing quality service. Walking away from this job was one of the hardest things I had to do because I loved the people I worked with as well as the clients. Due to corporate changes, I had to leave because I was no longer honoring my value of helping people. It is hard to provide quality service or a product to someone if you are constantly worrying about numbers and a strategy to bring in profits. When profit pressure is being constantly surfaced in different situations, it is easy to lose sight of your values.

One thing I have learned over the years, both professionally and personally, is that not everyone thinks like you or values the same things that you do. You may value treating people with respect and honor in order to get wealth, while a supervisor may value profit gains no matter how he has to treat people. After encountering this in various job settings throughout the years, I decided to become an entrepreneur and stay true to my authentic self and values. Is it hard some days? Yes! I have learned, during these times, that you must put on the value cap of creating wealth.

Value Cap

What is a value cap, you may be asking? A value cap is pulling out the values within to build wealth. As you know, my values are honesty, trust, authenticity, and respect. One day, as I was pondering my decision to become an entrepreneur, I created a value implementation plan that allowed me to do something I love. Professionally and personally I love to help people. I thought to myself, what better way to do this than building a business based on my core values?

Value Plan of Action

I would like to share the value plan of action that I created, which has worked a great deal for me. Before we move any further, though, I would like to briefly explain what an action plan is. An action plan is a format that allows you to plan tasks or goals that need to be achieved by setting a timeline for gaining wealth.

For example, if you love helping people, you'll need to develop a value action plan based upon those value ethics.

1. Trust Action Plan:
I will increase my clientele by two people in one month as a result of building a trusting relationship during my thirty-minute free call to an action consultation.

Follow-up: one client desired to move forward with service based on the values presented during consultation and on the connection made with the client during consultation.

<u>**Value-Based Wealth**</u>:
One client gained

• • •

2. Authenticity Action Plan:
I will demonstrate my honest love for helping people by providing quality services that embody respect, trust, and honesty.

Follow-up: Ask the client questions, or have her ask them of you, throughout the treatment.

Value-Based Wealth:
Client has a clear understanding of the treatment and values of my services.

Please take the time to develop your own personal and professional value plan of action based on the example above.

We have learned the background, basics, principles, and action plan of value. Now I would like to wrap everything up by providing tips for building wealth as an entrepreneur. It is important to always be thinking of ways to increase your profit.

The first step to building wealth is to determine how you can turn your values and passion into multiple streams of income. For example, you value painting because it allows people to enjoy the beauty of art. We have identified the value as well as how it contributes to society. Now let's look at how we can turn that love and value of art into multiple streams of income to build wealth.

As an artist, there can be several ways to build wealth. As an entrepreneur, you must be creative and expand upon your niche based on current trends and needs in addition to being proactive in developing strategies and solutions to become a valued wealth builder. For example:

- Teach art classes by contracting out with local schools and other organizations that focus on art as an acceleration of growth in one's self-identification.

- Create and paint personalized portraits for magazine covers. This particular idea for building wealth will also allow you to market yourself to thousands if your eye-catching portrait is featured in a top-rated magazine.

- Start an Art Birthday Party, hosting businesses where the theme of the party will be paintings that are based on the client's personal interest. Make it fun and unique, and be an irreplaceable party host.

Based on the example listed above, I would like to provide you with seven tips to build wealth based on value. I chose seven because the number signifies completion.

Value Tips to Build Wealth:

- Identify services or products that you need based on your personal and professional values.

- Partner with professionals who share the same values and create strategies and solutions for building wealth.

- Strategically develop a value-based action plan by developing a service or product that individually meets your value ethics.

- Provide training seminars and workshops that are based on your value.

- Expand on your values by increasing your knowledge base through academic enhancement or certification.

- Write a book.

- Journal to allow yourself to solely concentrate and create services and or products based upon your values.

In conclusion, having value to build wealth as an entrepreneur can be very rewarding; it is all about what you make it. Never lose sight of your value in anything you do, and always build your wealth on value because it is the right thing to do. I am truly humbled and blessed to have had the opportunity to share this valuable information with you on value and wealth. I pray that it blesses you in your personal and professional ventures.

"To value yourself outweighs the thoughts of society as long as you are being true to self."

Cyneta

8

Must Have Principle:

Money Management

LISA WILSON

We often dream of becoming rich, driving expensive cars, or taking a dream vacation, yet we never actually get down to business and begin the process of creating wealth. We sometimes think it is too hard to achieve, and then we begin to question ourselves as to whether we even have the knowledge or tools to get there. The simple truth is that making ourselves richer than we currently are is easier than ever before, with one caveat: There is no quick fix, and the process will take time and will require discipline for it to manifest. If you are like most people, you may have grown up being told that you have to work hard for the money.

Chances are good, however, that you may not have been told that it is also important to make your money work hard for you. It is no question that working hard for your money is important, but just working hard alone will not make you wealthy. How do I know that? Let's see, how many people do you know who work their butt off night and day and still are not wealthy?

This is why I have created a Roadmap for Wealth Strategies. A roadmap is a detailed plan to guide you toward your goal. We need a guide to help us stay on track with reaching our financial goals. I have listed the Roadmap for Wealth Strategies below:

- **Decisions, Decisions, Decisions:**
  You must first decide that you want to be wealthy and commit to do whatever is needed to create that wealth. Then define what exactly being wealthy means to YOU.

  How do you feel about wealth?

  What are your beliefs about wealth?

  What are your financial habits and traits?

  How confident are you in your ability to make financial decisions?

If you are not confident in your abilities to make a financial decision, are you willing to get help or educate yourself on the process? It is very important to have your own vision of wealth and a plan of action to reach your goals. If you don't know where you are going, I can assure you that you will never get there. This means holding absolutely nothing back and giving 100% of everything you have to achieve wealth.

It is time to be completely honest with yourself and become accountable for your financial future. If you have decided that you are comfortable with the questions above, I believe you are ready to move to the next step.

- **Your Past Does Affect Your Future:** The road to financial wealth does not begin in a bank or with a financial advisor. It starts in your head. It begins with your thoughts, and those thoughts, most times, will come from your past experiences with money.

I can even go so far to say that in my past experience as a bank manager, most of my client's struggles with money related back to their childhood experiences with it. I remember when I was about ten or eleven and my family lived in a two-story, three-bedroom house. My older sister and I shared a room, and my brother had a room to himself. One hot summer night, there was a knock at the door. I can remember my parents getting up and answering the door. I listened carefully to make sure that I did not miss what they were saying when they opened the door. I heard my oldest sister crying and saying to my parents that she had no place to go.

The next morning when I came downstairs my sister and her two children were asleep on the couch and floor. My mom was hushing me to be quiet and not wake them up. I could not understand why my sister was sleeping on the floor. What had happened that caused her to knock at the door late in the night and have to sleep on the floor? She has a home! Now she is on the floor at my parents' house. I asked my mom what happened to my oldest sister and her children, and she explained to me that my sister would be staying with us for a little while because she had lost her home and needed to find a new one. I did not realize how this experience would later affect my future.

It was just my sister falling on hard times and moving home, after all. I later discovered that this experience had a dramatic effect on my future.

You see, I had made up in my mind that this would never happen to me! I always said that once I moved out, I would never move back home. I did not want to put more pressure on my parents. Without my knowing it, this memory played itself out well into my adult years. For many years, even though I was becoming more successful, I continued to have this fear of having to move back home with my family, being on the other side of that door at my parents' house like my sister had been. Not being good enough to be independent for the rest of my life, but there was a small thought that I would fail. This created inconsistency in how I managed my business and finances.

I was always second-guessing myself and did not have the full confidence that I could succeed. Messages about money are passed down from generation to generation. Your own personal memories about money will tell you a lot, if you step back and think about those

Cultivating Your IT Factor

past experiences and what they have taught you and whether those memories are still telling you who you are today.

Try this: I want you to complete an exercise with me.

Look back into your childhood and remember everything you can about money—the wonderful things it did and the ways in which it may have scared you. After you have spent some time completing this exercise and allowing these memories to flow, begin to write down everything about that memory that you can remember. Face your past so you can embrace your future.

_____

_____

_____

_____

Simple smart goals: Setting financial goals can assist you in creating your dream life. In fact, research states that setting goals improves your performance across every area of your life, whether you want to lose weight or save more money.

Use the SMART method to create actionable goals. SMART is a mnemonic terminology used by motivators, educators, and corporations as a system of goal identification, setting, and achievement. Every letter in SMART stands for an adjective that describes an effective way to set your personal goals.

- ✓ **Specific** – Target a specific area that you want improvement in.

- ✓ **Measurable** – Establish concrete criteria to measure your progress.

- ✓ **Attainable** – Make sure the goal is within your reach.

- ✓ **Relevant** – Make the goal realistic and reasonable.
- ✓ **Time-Related** – Give enough time to achieve the goal.

Turn each goal into a positive statement. Using positive statements will assist you in affirming your commitment so you can complete your goals. Set priorities, and then decide which goals are more important or time sensitive. Keep track of your progress by writing your goals down in a journal or notebook. Checking in with yourself and acknowledging your progress will help you make better goals and staying more motivated.

Reward yourself for your accomplishments. Acknowledge yourself when you have reached your goal, and allow yourself to celebrate.

Create a budget: Creating a budget is a practical way to get a grip on your spending. Creating a budget can help you identify how you spend money, plan for your future, pay off existing debt, and save. It can also help you to evaluate your current spending habits and assist you in setting goals that take into account your long-term financial needs. Categorize your expenses by setting up a monthly budget and start with the big categories first before breaking down the smaller ones.

Within each general budget category, some items are essential (mortgage or rent payments, utility bills, and groceries); others are extra (gifts, purses, and makeup). Look through the list and find flexible budget expenses that you may be able to cut back on. Put a check mark next to those flexible items so you can identify them. Estimate what it is you spend each month. Go through your checkbook and receipts to see what exactly you are spending money on. It is important to look at the big picture and start a budget by cutting expenses.

Pay yourself first: This phrase is commonly used in personal finance and retirement planning material, and it means to automatically route your specified savings contribution from your paycheck at the time it is received. Because savings contributions are automatically routed from your paycheck to your investment account, this process is what it means to "pay yourself first." In other words, you pay yourself before you begin paying your monthly living expenses and making purchases. It removes the temptation to skip a given month's contribution and the risk of spending the funds before the contribution has been made to your account. Regular and consistent savings contributions can go a long way toward building a long-term nest egg. When you "pay yourself first," you are mentally establishing your savings as a priority. You are telling yourself that you are more important than your utility company or landlord.

Building a savings is a powerful motivator and it is also empowering. "Paying yourself first" encourages sound financial habits, and the best way to develop a saving habit is to make the process as painless as possible. Make it automatic, make it invisible, and make it attainable. If you have arranged to have your money taken out of your paycheck before you receive it, you will never know it is missing. If your employer offers a retirement plan such as a 401k plan, you need to enroll as soon as possible, especially if the company matches your contribution.

Matched contributions are like getting free money. Open a high-interest savings account at your local or online bank. Set up automatic transfers into this account, either directly from your paycheck or from your bank account. This should be your first and most important bill that needs to be paid every month. I believe everyone can save at least 1%

of their income. That is only one penny out of every dollar.

If you find yourself struggling to save money, consider setting aside your next raise for the future and continue to cut expenses. As your income begins to increase, set your goals aside for retirement and savings. Establishing this habit early on can lead to increased financial security later in your life.

Money, Money, Money (Passive Income): Are you hoping to one day make enough money from your current job so that you can retire? If this is the case, you might want to rethink your plan. Things have changed from the days of our parents and grandparents. In those days, you could work for the same company for 30-40 years and retire comfortably. This is no longer the case due to fewer corporate job benefits and lower wages. While your 8-5 job may be enough to pay your basic bills, it may not be enough to pay into your retirement. The solution may be found in creating passive income. Think of passive income as residual income streams that keep on flowing. Your salary, commission, and any bonuses are called active income because they are received for services or labor rendered. Our society does not place much emphasis on making passive income. We are taught to work 40 plus years, and then try to retire based on active income. This may work for some, but the majority of the population will not be able to retire on active income alone.

Generating passive income means letting your money work for you. It does not require you to be directly involved in earning the income. This will free you up to be able to accomplish other things while your money continues to grow for you. If your passive income does not make you rich, it can help with other things, such as making car payments or credit card payments, or help you pay off debt sooner. I've listed four possible passive income streams below:

1. **Affiliate marketing** – Sign up with a company and sell their products either through a website, email marketing system, and or social media.

2. **Network marketing** – Also called multi-level marketing (MLM), this is another way to earn passive income.

When you join a network marketing company, you become part of a team. If you have good leaders that know how to build and develop people and teams, you could be successful.

3. **Become a Virtual Assistant** – Today VAs can do just about any job for you that does not require for them to be in a physical office. The best VAs can earn $30-$50 per hour.

4. **Take Paid Surveys at Home** – Companies are desperately wanting your opinion and they are willing to pay for your opinion. The key is to find a survey company that pays the best. One of the popular online survey companies is CASHCRATE.

To summarize, you can achieve wealth over time, and if you follow the Roadmap to Wealth Strategy steps, I believe you will have great success. Good Luck!

Lisa

9

Must Have Principle:

Lifestyle Balance

MINISTER NELLIE ANITA WOSU

Lifestyle balance, or work-life balance, is on the move. We hear about it even in the halls of Corporate America. Often, we seek employment based on how a particular corporation is able to find a good work-life balance, using it to determine whether we want to be a candidate in their hallowed corridors. At just about every turn of life, and in every arena, we come face to face with the work-life balance conundrum. Do you believe this? If so, why? And if not, why?

One of the reasons we find this truth difficult to accept is because of our inability to make a firm decision and stick with it. Everything is done outside of the home today. However, everything is seemingly done from the palm of our hands and the tip of our index fingers.

Yes, the hand! The hand, which is that marvelous digitized creation that Adam extends to God, is one of the greatest depictions of life balance and understanding made by the quintessential master artist himself, Michelangelo.

Michelangelo painted that entire scene on the ceiling of the Sistine Chapel between 1508 and 1512. What does that have to do with us today, here in the 21st century? More than one would perhaps realize, care to know, or even fathom. We have a myriad of choices each day that swamps us with opportunities to move up or get out of jail for free. Is freedom ever an option? How is it that a painting of epic proportions created centuries ago even remotely speaks to our lifestyle balance today?

I tell you, it speaks volumes about the nature of us and the nature of God. Without God, there is no nature and there never will be. From God, all nature is bountifully given. There is no lack in God and there never will be.

Our nature drives us for more. The ability to obtain more, want more, and, at times, unfortunately, to destroy more.

Don't get me wrong, I'm not a fatalist. It is my desire to garner as much positivity as possible in any situation. As maturity sets up residence in me over these nearly 55 years that I've been present on Earth, I've discarded many notions about what actually sustains my being. One of those notions that I have discarded is that I need to do everything for everyone all the time. No, I actually do not need to do that. I'm not a gambling person, but I bet the same is apropos for you as well, even if you haven't lived yet to be two nickels!

The individual in relationship with one's Creator is the single most essential lifestyle balance that one can have or need. I also truly believe that one does not have to be "religious" to embrace this truth. I've found that religiosity destroys relationships unwittingly at times.

Michelangelo's creation of Adam has always made me wonder why he painted the rendering on the ceiling of the chapel. That must have been a daunting endeavor. The ceiling is way up in the air. It's not a low ceiling. The work is intricate, by far. The luxury of scaffolding that we take for granted in our technologically driven world was not vogue in that day. As previously noted, the painting was created over many years, painstakingly at that. I bet, at times, Michelangelo was on his back painting that truth of Adam and God, inspired by his spirit within him, to focus on his relationship with God.

As I mentioned above, we live our lives daily from the palm of our hand, carrying those insidious devices everywhere we go. They demand our attention, and we respond with our pointer fingers (index finger), ready to do whatever needs to be done. They have become our God, seemingly. Is that what is deemed a significant lifestyle balance?

Lifestyle balance has more to do with personal relationships than it does with an Infiniti M35, BMWs, Benz, Lexus, five-bedroom house, three-car garage, or even an Ivy League education, corner office, and three vacations per year. Of course, let's not also forget the ubiquitous 401K noose that hangs around our collective neck.

I am for open commerce, domestic and international. I do believe in our ability to grow and to do more with less, but, at the same time, I am pro-heart. I am pro-love and pro-true relationships, especially those that exist in your own heart-space with your Lord. For without that key and essential relationship, there will never, ever be any tangible endeavor that will matter or succeed.

Our lifestyle balance must begin and end with a true purpose of dedicated time with God, the Father, Jesus the Christ, and the Holy Spirit in order to find your lifestyle balance. You've known and heard for quite some time that life is about what you put into it. Absolutely. I agree.

Life is God. All life is of and from God, our source. We will not achieve even a semblance of balance if we remain out of balance in life. We've been given an opportunity to bring out change within our own personal sphere of relationship. First things first, always. You want to achieve greatness? Yes, many of us do. For that greatness you want to achieve, have you taken the matter up with your CEO, the Lord? Is that what you want, or is that what He wants for you? Oh yes, and does that greatness you want to achieve glorify your Lord? Will it assist in Kingdom building? Will it reach out to the heart of another individual and uplift, encourage, and inspire her to build a better foundational standard for her new lifestyle balance living within the realm of Christ? I am an achiever from way back. I greatly desire to do more for others and less for myself. You see, I've attained all that I need to succeed. It has been freely given to me. I now seek to expand from the inside out.

What I have attained is through going within my "self" to see who I am and not what a survey says I am. I've asked my God, "Who is this woman/child you've created me to be? What is your purpose for her?" He led me to Matthew 6:33. I will not include the scripture for you here, with the hopes that you will seek it out on your own. When you're ready to read it, you'll be in perfect balance, and your life and style will speak volumes for you. You will simply do as Jesus told the man: "Don't say anything, just go and show yourself."

Show yourself to be dedicated to the one who is able to do exceedingly and abundantly more than you could ever ask. I promise you, you'll find that the balance you've achieved, even when the winds of life and change come to destroy your balance and toss you to and fro, you'll know, within your deepest and innermost places that is always enlightened, that the peace you seek is yours and no one can steal or take it away from you, ever. Recently, I wrote on a piece of paper during a challenging day that "aging is not for wimps." And, it's not! Aging calls for one to be accountable for one's own self, good, bad, or otherwise. Old folks would say that when you know that you know, you know.

Step away from everything that places demands on your being, and decide if it's what you need to be doing right now. And do as Michelangelo's Adam did to God. He, Adam, stretched his hand to God. God's hand is always extended to us. Shall we stretch and extend our heart and entire being to Him for His glory? When, and if, we choose to do so, just know that is the beginning of a lifestyle balance beyond compare.

It is my prayer that you will seek balance in mind, body, spirit, and soul so you can achieve more through your obedience to the clarion call upon your life. Everyone doesn't need to be a CEO of their own enterprise. We simply need to be willing workers in the vineyard, and when we are that, He alone will provide the desires of the heart that He keeps eternally for His own. Then you will have achieved lifestyle balance. And, oh what a life it will be! If He did it for me, He'll do it for you too!

I Am The Encouraging One!

John 3:2 New King James Version (NKJV)

2 This man came to Jesus by night and said to Him, "Rabbi, we know that You are a teacher come from God; for no one can do these signs that You do unless God is with him."

3 John 1:2 New King James Version (NKJV)

2 Beloved, I pray that you may prosper in all things and be in health, just as your soul prospers.

Minister Wosu

10

Must Have Principle:

Stress Relief

MISTE M. ANDERS–CLEMONS

No matter what plight we may have in life—rich or poor, male or female, married or single, parents or no parents—one guarantee is that we will all face some sort of stress, even if what may be stressful to one person may not be stressful to another.

"Stress is poison." – Agavé Powers

1. The Early Years and Stress

Children sometimes as young as five years old can and will deal with stress. How they deal with it at that point can create a baseline for them when they become adults. Most children are ill-equipped to handle stress or even know what stress is.

Case in point, as a young athlete at 12 years old, I was going to a Junior Olympic event representing my state as a track and field runner. I was very excited and yet scared at the same time. I was fine until I got there and became very stressed out. Suddenly, my knee blew up like it had water in it so I was unable to compete.

This was my first dramatic experience with stress as a young person and led me to understand some things about how I responded to stress.

Years after that, I realized that I internalized stress. I had been calm, cool, and collected on the outside, but on the inside I was freaking out, and my body responded with water under the knee. This was my first major experience with high levels of stress.

Our parents and teachers try as they might to prepare us for life, but they don't really prepare us for stress. Thus, this becomes a battle we need to discover and fight on our own. We have a history with stress, and it begins in our younger years.

• • • TIME TO DESTRESS

Questions:

1) What was your first experience with stress that you can vividly recall?

2) What age were you, and how did you respond?

Exercise:
Create a timeline of your life from birth to present and mark major stressful events in the timeline.

Affirmation:
I choose now to learn and grow from my stress, creating a life of calm and tranquility.

Quote:
"Stress is the trash of modern life—we all generate it but if you don't dispose of it properly, it will pile up and overtake your life." – Terri Guillemets

2. From Stress to More Stress
What we may find in life is that we are going from stress to more stress. Similar to muscles that get stronger when you work them out or

challenge them with more weights, stress, too, can be very stressful in our teen years and may be only minor as an adult. So, as we go through life and get older, we become more in tune with ourselves as well as with our stressors. We become better adapted at assessing potential stress. We have a better idea of the things we find relaxing and that help us in stressful moments.

Approximately 10 years after my knee injury, I went to college and found myself in another track and field competition on a national level, representing my college. The stakes were high. At that time, I was a student in college and a wife, holding down at least two part-time jobs to finance my education. I was also an owner of a martial arts studio with my husband.

Amazingly, due to a multitude of stresses that I had been through in the past years, this did not stress me out. I was under a little stress, but nothing like before. Through the course of life situations and circumstances that I have gone through, I can operate and be under more stress than I was in times past.

• • • TIME TO DESTRESS

Questions:

1) In what ways have I gone from stress to more stress?

2) Would I also be described as having stronger stress muscles at that point in time?

Exercise:
Look at and write down the ways in which you have unsuccessfully and successfully dealt with stress in your life.

Affirmation:
I choose to develop my stress muscles and be stronger and stronger with each passing moment.

Quote:
"Stress is not what happens to us. It's our response TO what happens. And RESPONSE is something we can choose." – Maureen Killoran

3. What is stress to you?
Just as we are each unique individuals, stress, too, can be unique. Something may be exceedingly

stressful to one person, and yet to another it might be a walk in the park. To give some examples, my dad was in Vietnam as a medic, and I cannot imagine in my wildest dreams how stressful that could have been.

Let's say, for example, that I expressed to my dad my frustrations with the classes I was taking in college, and that it was difficult to pass them. My dad was very sensitive to my plight, but compared to what he may have endured during war, my educational endeavors were probably to him a walk in the park.

As a teenager, I lived in Dorchester, Massachusetts, which is often described as a "tough neighborhood." As a person living there, going to school, hanging out with my friends, and jogging through the streets, it was the environment I knew, and I was used to having to watch my back and being extremely vigilant at all times. So for me, this was not necessarily stressful, but simply my day-to-day life. I was used to the inner city way of living. A few years later, my family and I moved to Marston Mills, Massachusetts, which was totally the opposite.

Marston Mills was a suburb and had a small population. With my previous mindset and experience, Marston Mills was a walk in the park.

• • • TIME TO DESTRESS

Questions:

1) At this point and time in your life, what are your low-level stress items?

2) What are your high-level stress items?

Exercise:
Review what items in your life tend to cause you to feel stressed. Is there a trend in your stressful moments? Are there "hot buttons" of stress that you experience?

Affirmation:
No matter what my "hot button" is, I will be proactive and not reactive.

Quote:
"It's not stress that kills us, it is our reaction to it." Hans Selye

4. What does stress feel like to you?
It's important to be aware of what stress feels like to you so you can head it off at the pass.

One of the major aspects of stress is that people don't know what it feels like. When I was pregnant with my first child, I had no idea what to expect, or how pregnancy would feel on me, what labor would be like, or even what a contraction was. Sure enough, almost nine months later, I had all the answers to my questions, and I also had a baseline.

Even though it would be almost a decade later before I had my second child, I still knew the basics of pregnancy. It is similar with stress. If when I experience stress I recall and remember what I am feeling, what emotions are going on, and what is going in my body, then I become aware. When you are aware of how something affects you emotionally and physically, you can then counteract.

• • • TIME TO DESTRESS

Questions:

1) When I am going through stress what does my body feel like?

2) How would you describe stress?

3) If stress had a color what would it be?

4) Where does it resonate in your body?

Exercise:
If you were to draw or illustrate your stress, what would it look like? What colors would it consist of?

Affirmation:
I choose to be aware of stress around and within me and also choosing serenity and peacefulness.

Quote:
"Give your stress wings and let it fly away."
Terri Guillemets

5. Have a De-Stress Daily Plan:

As in all things, it is important if not imperative, to have a plan. A famous saying says, "If you don't plan, you plan to fail." It is the same with stress. As a former athlete, I trained, did weights, and worked with my coaches to plan for championships, which led to becoming an All-American in track and field. When pregnant with my children, I also developed and had a "birth plan," and I attended Lamaze classes to prepare for labor.

Even as an entrepreneur, you must develop a business plan, review your product offerings, and constantly review your financials. Look at what you can plan on doing to help yourself. It is important to have a plan for various environments you may be in at any given day. Create a stress-less plan for home, work, the commute, or weekends.

Your Stress-Less Living Plan may include the following:

Praying	Walking	Meditating
Bible Study	Hiking	Journaling
Reading	Jogging/Running	Cooking/Baking
Writing	Coloring/ Drawing	Watching TV
Music	Deep breathing	Crafting
Painting	Day dreaming	Swimming
Dancing	Talking	Cleaning
Fishing	Yoga/Pilates	Taking a nap
Playing videos games	Going to the movies	Being around children

• • • TIME TO DESTRESS

Questions: What if integrated a Stress-Less Living Plan into my life? Would it successfully help me with stress?

1) At home?

2) At work?

Exercise:
Develop a plan of action on a daily basis to help keep stress at bay.

Affirmation:
I have successfully developed a plan that will assist me in managing stress daily.

Now that you have developed your own "de-stressing plan," place your top five to ten actions that you can do in these situations and circumstances, from tending to your home and job to commuting, and put them on index cards or on your phone as reminders for things that you can turn to in order to distress.

Place them on your refrigerator, bathroom mirror, or in your bedroom. Put them in your cubicle, in a nice frame, or on your weekly calendar. On your commute you can have it on an index card, in the console area of your car, or on your phone as a recording.

6. Stressful Situations and Circumstances: For other situations in your life that you may find yourself in, place your cards in designated areas to also help you. It is very important to be on the lookout at all times and it is especially important to create plans for various times of your life where stress, good and bad, is possible and prone to creep in. Being unplanned at these times can cause setbacks that you could have prepared for ahead of time. Some of the situations and circumstances that you may need to be on the lookout for are:

Interviewing	Social situations	Divorce/ Separation
First day on the job	Family additions	Weddings/ Marriage
Job loss	Family loss	New relationships
Client loss	Going to school	Moving
Financial increases/ decreases	Children attending school	Medical procedures for you or other

Be prepared and have a plan at ALL times, and things will be less likely to take you by storm.

CALM IN CHAOS:

"In the midst of the flurry – clarity. In the midst of the storm – calm. In the midst of divided interests – certainty. In the many roads – a certain choice. " – Mary Anne Radmache.

Choose calm, peace, centeredness, tranquility, stillness, and serenity.

Miste

11

Must Have Principle:

Healthy Self-Concept

ALAINA ODESSA

*a*side from God, your self-image is the most powerful abstract thing in your life. Although you never see it, it bears your constant reflection, reflecting who you perceive yourself to be through other people's eyes. And because nothing can be experienced outside the filter of self-image, however conscious of you that you are is the lens through which you are always looking.

Self-image is the frame you have used to put yourself together. It is inside that frame that you have hung your sense of self.

Even if the literal words are never voiced, your sense of self makes continual subconscious declarations like:

Cultivating Your IT Factor

- I am good vs. I am wrong
- I am wanted vs. I am not wanted
- I belong vs. I am alone
- I am enough vs. I am inferior
- I am capable vs. I am a failure
- I am safe vs. I am insecure
- I am seen vs. I am invisible
- I am powerful vs. I am a victim

The permission you give yourself in life and in your brand to:

- Be or not be
- Do or not do
- Have or not have
- Try or deny
- Connect or fly alone
- Explore or stay confined

All these states and more are determined and defined by the way you see yourself. Who you've learned to believe you are, and what you've been taught to believe you can have and do has become your mindset, set by the experiences you've had with others. THIS is what governs your life and your brand! Self-image is THE most powerful force that dominates a woman's quality of life.

And yet, as powerful as it is, it's also the most vulnerable and susceptible. Here's why: You shape your self-image, but you did so according to others. Self-image is the portrait we draw of ourselves according to who we've learned to believe we are based on the influences and interactions experienced in the culture and environment we are reared in.

What that means is this: Our self-image is totally responsible for governing every aspect of how we allow ourselves to live, love, and do business in the world, and yet it's something we create when we are still unaware and unsuspecting little girls! I know, right? Wild. But at the same time, our understanding of what self-image is and how it works begins to break down and explain where all those feelings of emptiness, craziness, double-mindedness, and "stuckness" are really coming from. The clarity gives us a new perspective and power in our relationships, including the ones we have with our business and our brand. When we understand based on source, we have the power to transform the root.

A Little of My Story

It took me decades, a loving God, and lots of inner work to cultivate the courage I needed to step out of the wreckage of my damaged identity and into a personal peace with the person God created me to BE. If it weren't for His Word and our relationship, I'd be way worse off than crazy. I truly believe that I'd be dead, and I CERTAINLY believe I wouldn't have been equipped to birth a brand and develop a business.

See, I spent girlhood constructing a self-concept framed by contradictions. If I'd had a brand back then, it would have been called the Scatter Brand because a sense of security was my primary need, and I morphed into whoever I felt I had to be to get it. I grew up wanting to be an actress. It was so secret, though, that I didn't tell myself until I was 33 years old, safe in the arms of God. But here's the thing: We're such natural creators that I never realized I'd made a production of my life, cast myself in all the roles, and played my parts perfectly. Like the little girl in me who crafted the production blindly, the woman, just as blind, never saw herself in the act. I didn't know that my inner child was running the show, and I certainly had no idea that I could take the reigns from her hands.

But I see so clearly now, how I cast myself in role after role, dumbed myself down, and pretended not to see what was going on in my relationships with men, money, gifts, inclinations, and interests. "The ditz," by definition, doesn't take responsibility for her life or her hopes and heart's desires. So as long as I spoke from her lines, I continued in the false belief that no real damage was being done.

I played the role of "good consumer," bought all the trappings earned from the good government job that I had kept for years, even though I hated it. Clothes, shoes, purses, cars, and the best little house stuffed with all the stuffings that my misery money could buy. My life looked awesome from the curb, but inside, emptiness ate me alive like a cancer.

My diseased self-image was governing me to make unhealthy choices in every area of life, and then it held me hostage to live with the results. Even as my diseased identity strangled my spirit, it demanded that I continue to put on my game face and play the role of "I'm fine." I ache just remembering those times. I was exhausted and sick by the end.

I completely lacked the energy to even crawl up to anyone's altar. I remember that that night, I somehow rolled my body, itching and clammy, off the side of the bed and fell to the floor, wailing and begging God both to hear me and to be who I'd heard He was.

Going into that night, I had zero understanding of what salvation was. Sure, I'd confessed Christ as Savior and Lord in my 20s, but that had been about church. That night, the naked, wailing need that I was asking God to clothe was about life. Thank God, He came. Or was He already there? All I know is that my process of transformation had begun. And not just me—my brand and I were born again that night. All my work and intentions are now filtered through seeing and recognizing myself as a woman of God called to help born-again women everywhere BLOOM by cultivating a healthy, whole, and healed self-image.

BE Ye Transformed By The Renewing of Your Mind.

Some scriptures in the Bible are quoted so often that even non-believers know them. I call them "scriptures we've quoted the fire out of." They've been traditionalized to the point that they're hardly really *heard* anymore. Romans 12:2 can make that list if we're not careful. Here it is from the New King James Version:

And do not be conformed to this world, but be transformed by the renewing of your mind, that you may prove what is that good and acceptable and perfect will of God.

Submitting to the process of renewing our minds isn't a mere suggestion, not for those who actually desire to see the good, acceptable, and perfect will of God be proven through the work of their lives and brand. It's a command. It's not a "we should" command, but rather a "we get to" command.

There's such an awesome promise of deliverance in Romans 12:2. When we receive it in the fullness of its vitality, we find ourselves saying "yes" to a glorious new beginning where we actually start to experience the possibilities and wonder of our Christian inheritance.

Saying "yes" to Romans 12:2 positions us to be able to reach out and receive the divine rescue rope that has come to pull us free from the worldly snare of a diseased self-image.

The consummation and fulfillment of everything we want for ourselves, for our brand and business, every hope and dream we have for those clients sent to us to invest in themselves through us is birthed again and again through our courage and willingness to discover the truth and beauty of our own God-made selves. Honestly, successful brands and businesses are nothing more than additional expressions of a healthy self-image.

We're blessed to share it with others. And it's when we accept the call to commit to, and continue in, the pursuit of being taken from self-image glory to God's glory, and that we can truly bless our brand, our clients, ourselves, and our God.

Dominion

Dominion speaks to ruler-ship, jurisdiction, power, and authority. God gave you dominion so that you would be made of God.

Genesis 1:26a reads:

And God said, Let us make man in our image, to be like us. Let them have dominion...

That's straight from the throne. And what it suggests is this:

- You may have learned that you lack this or that.

- You may have been conditioned to seek approval and acceptance before making big moves.

- You may have allowed others to train you to dim your light.

- You may have trained yourself to believe that there's a limit on your brand's growth.

But the truth is you are a child of the Most High God. Nothing is impossible for you.

YOU HAVE BEEN GIVEN DOMINION! Dominion over your life, over your mind, over your self-concept.

YOUR IDENTITY BELONGS TO YOU!

You can make a decision right now to walk in your God-given dominion, to develop and mature it so you can start actively and intentionally creating a life that you love—one that glorifies and honors God, proving His good, acceptable, and perfect will. Whatever you desire, beloved, you have the authority to create. Be it personal, professional, relational, financial, creative, or spiritual; if it pertains to you, you have both dominion and rule over it.

Self-Image Is the Frame

Self-image is the frame that holds the contents of your life. Now that we've reiterated what it is, how it functions, and how it is 100 percent susceptible to your leadership and intention, now that we've reiterated the fact that you have both authority, dominion, and access to the wisdom you need to build a new and better frame, what will you do?

Will you intentionally build your self-image on the rock of the Word of God, believing that you are who God says you are, are able to do what God says you can do, and can have what God says you can have for your life and for your business?

Refuse to live another day subservient to the falsehood and brokenness of how you have learned to see yourself and your potential through the eyes of a fallen world.

God has given you the desires of your heart. He's poured the oil of anointing upon your head, and He's impregnated you with the ability to manifest and mature in your purpose and in every promise that's been spoken in your spirit. Your enemies can't stop it; a fluctuating economy can't stop it; an unstable government can't; not limited education or contacts; and now, not even an ill-informed self-image. *Nothing* on this earth has the power to stop you from manifesting the plans and purposes that God has created and placed you in the earth to BE, do, and have.

A healthy, whole, and healed self-image is part of your salvation package. It is part of your inheritance as a believer in, and confessor of, Christ Jesus.

Practices to Cultivate a Healthy Self Image

You can use any or all of these five proven practices to cultivate a healthy self-image that will serve you in the creation, cultivation, and growth of a powerful brand.

1. Meditation.

Joshua 1:8 (NIV) Keep this Book of the Law always on your lips. Meditate on it day and night so you will be sure to obey everything written in it. Only then will you prosper and succeed in all you do.

The word "meditate" means "to mutter; speak softly to oneself; to imagine and ponder over; to sit with; commune with and consider." However you define it, meditation will renew your mind and help you prosper in your intended purpose.

2. Confessions/Declarations.

Job 22:28 (NKJV) You will also declare a thing, and it will be established for you; so light will shine on your ways.

God presented animals to Adam to see what he would call them, and God is doing the same with you. What you call something is what it's going to be. Carve out time to intentionally use your words to create the life, experience, and brand you desire to have.

3. Study.

2 Timothy 2:15 (KJV) Study to show thyself approved unto God, a workman that needeth not to be ashamed, rightly dividing the word of truth.

Reading and studying are not things we graduated from when we finished the last days of high school, college, independent study, or post-graduate studies. When you study, you enrich and expand your level of possibility. Commit to studying at least two hours per week and to reading at least 30 minutes before you sleep.

4. Visualizing/Imagining.

Genesis 15:5 (NLT) Then the Lord took Abram outside and said to him, "Look up into the sky and count the stars if you can. That's how many descendants you will have!"

You've heard that iron sharpens iron. Imagine that self-image and imagination are two iron anvils striking against one another to make the other sharper. Active, intentional, and creative use of your imagination WILL enlarge and expand your territory.

5. Writing / Journaling.

Habakkuk 2:2 (NKJV) Write the vision and make it plain on tablets, that he may run who reads it.

Computers and tablets are now in competition with good old-fashioned writing, but physical writing is a spiritual act. Set an intention to write something personal every day.

6. Self-Pursuit.
(personal outings/adventures/discovery)

Philippians 2:13 (NKJV) For it is God Who works in you both to will and to do for His good pleasure.

Get to know yourself better through intentional self-exploration. If you're curious about it, do it. If you're wondering, try it. If it interests you, make a commitment to honor yourself by simply checking it out.

Seed, Time and Harvest... Be patient with yourself. Genesis 8:22 lets us know that while the earth remains, seedtime and harvest shall not cease. Your self-image has and will continue to develop over time.

The vision and conceptualization of your brand has been, and will continue to, develop over time as well.

Be patient, yet intentional, around your process of development. Trust that you are not only cultivating your "it" factor, but that you're doing a stellar job of that. Be gentle with the crop called YOU because YOU are amongst the most precious and valuable crops in the Kingdom. I pray you see yourself that way more every day!

Alaina

12

Must Have Principle:

Signature Presence

CHERRI WALSTON

Showcasing your personal style does not mean grandstanding or enlisting a PR firm; it means being visible in a crowded marketplace with a unique twist that showcases you, your brand.

It will require you to make a shift in how you see yourself and your perspective, forcing you to let go of what you know as the traditional concept of brand.

In today's highly competitive business landscape, it is very important to use tools that are available online to enhance your online brand visibility, reach, and exposure. Blending your personal style with your passion business (a business about a cause or problem you know you can solve that invigorates you on a cellular level) and getting your message to the masses is critical to your entrepreneurial success. One of the biggest challenges that most enterprising women face is how to get noticed and stand out in a sea of clamoring entrepreneurs who are seeking clients, customers, profits, and recognition. Sometimes you can feel like a little guppy surrounded in a pool of sharks. The good news is that you can be a little fish in a BIG pond with your signature style and consistent message spread across various technological platforms and networks.

"Social Proof" is a term used to indicate how people make buying decisions based on reviews, comments, and likes across social and online media platforms. That trustability stems from the way you show up on various social platforms that people experience you through.

I vividly remember that when I started my coaching business, there was a sea of other coaches doing exactly what I wanted to do. I felt like I was competing and doing the same thing. I wondered how I would get clients and whether my ideal clients would see me differently and want to work with me. I had no signature style that said who I was and what I stood for. I was just another look-alike vying for a piece of the pie. It took me several years with the right coach and mentor to figure out my personal style and message that would set me apart from the masses in my industry. My authentic and sassy style, along with my new brand message, afforded me a bigger pond to swim in using various media platforms to become more visible and more credible. The traditional way of branding via the yellow pages, newspaper, TV, and radio have morphed into an online presence.

In my experience as a corporate professional and entrepreneur, I have found that the five most important online tools of value to any enterprising woman are: Google, Facebook, Fiverr, LinkedIn, and YouTube. Each of these valuable tools can be leveraged to tell your brand message online and create consistent brand awareness across multiple platforms. The best way to achieve the vision you have for your business online is to infuse your personal style and signature message so that you are building a presence that spotlights your uniqueness.

These may seem intimidating when you are first starting out in your business, but in time you will get the hang of them and be able to navigate them with ease and confidence. The cool thing about these platforms is that they have little to no cost.

As a new entrepreneurial woman building a business while working, you don't have to break your bank account to start a business. Once you create your signature message and infuse your personal style that attracts, magnetizes, and captives your ideal audience while using social media and outsourcing services to help, you will stand out. Before setting out in your entrepreneurial venture to navigate the vast online landscape, it is vital that you understand that when people search by name, product, and service online, in order to differentiate yourself you have to create the IT factor. You want to have that pleasant quality that cannot be adequately described or expressed. In other words, you want people to think that there's no other person like you.

You have made your personal and signature style stand out among your peers in the noisy marketplace. Knowing how to present yourself online takes courage and confidence in who you are, so you can create what is called "likeability" by each network or platform with which you list or submit your brand, business, or website.

I shied away from social media because I didn't understand how it worked in leveraging a personal brand. Well, initially, too, I didn't understand what a brand really was. Not until I worked with a branding expert, at least. I had to revamp everything I knew and had been doing for years. I was struggling in my business to get noticed. And when I learned how to show up on social platforms with a clear message and brand, infusing my personal style, people began to take notice. I made significant connections and business contacts that led to increased profitability. I had people searching for me and taking notice of my new brand. I was now establishing social proof.

How to create the IT Factor with your online presence

One of the keys to having a great online presence is to make your ideal clients or customers notice you in a way that makes him or her want to buy your products and services. Your presence and likeability has more to do with consistent data being accurate on all platforms and networks, as well as with the understanding that likeability leads to further enhancement of social proof. Google, Facebook, LinkedIn, and YouTube are all tools that can help you build your social proof, which will change your business and lend itself as viable. Fiverr.com, too, is a tool you can use to create content, images, video, etc.

Building your social proof is done through reviews, likes, endorsements, and shares of the aforementioned networks in order to monetize your personal brand.

Using these five tools can help you leverage your entrepreneurial venture, signature style, and personal brand with ease and consistency. These are the things I call your "low hanging fruit"; they are especially easy and are free or low cost tools for someone building an entrepreneurial dream while working and on a small budget.

Google
Google My Business is a new tool that I stumbled upon that can help you promote your brand, products, and services. It is a great way to manage your online presence. This tool connects you to entrepreneurs or business owners with customers by starting a conversation with your ideal clients or customers. Whether they're looking for you on search maps or Google +, using Google My Business

helps you show up on Google and gives customers and clients the right information about your business so you can build relationships that last. When you provide your customers and clients with accurate information about your personal brand, remember to make it so that your customers can participate in enhancing the growth and development of your brand and business.

Facebook

This is, by far, my favorite vehicle for getting noticed and building social proof. If you use it correctly, with the purpose and mission of enhancing your brand and establishing a following, you will see growth and build online visibility and credibility. Creating a Facebook Fan Page for your business gives you the opportunity to showcase your personal style and brand in a way that has a large impact online. This means that your brand and business can leverage and engage a liked-minded audience by posting quotes, questions, videos, and photos that connect with your brand message as well as the service you offer. By engaging your audience, you increase the likelihood of your fans sharing your information.

Cultivating Your IT Factor

Your personal Facebook page can work in the same way; you just need to make sure you know what your intent is, because either way you are still branding yourself. Now Facebook Groups are more about forming a community of interest and specific focus or movement. You can create momentum with this by sharing your vision, brand message, and cause, using it as a platform to host your services.

Fiverr.com
This service is an unbeatable value for anyone starting out in her business for something that is beyond her scope, expertise, or skill. You can get services such as a virtual assistant, website, video editing, logos, banners, content writing and more for $5+. This is excellent for anyone starting out without a lot of money, especially since you do need administrative services so you can focus more on building your brand and personal style. Fiverr.com is inexpensive and can help create social proof with various services that enhance your business and brand. It is one of the best services I have found and used to sharpen my brand with graphics that reflect my personal

style and brand and to promote my offerings. You can also work with as many contractors for your services as you like. I have found a few that I use on a consistent basis because they understand my personal style and they are able to create exactly what I need.

As you are starting out as a working woman, building a business with the desire to transition into a full-time entrepreneur, you'll need to remember that your personal brand is key to creating an attraction and following for growing your business. Develop your brand message and signature style so you don't fall into the track of a copycat. Instead, develop a brand that creates social buzz across various platforms and enhances your brand, influencing the buying decisions of your ideal customers or clients to buy your products and services.

Personal Style and Social Proof Checklist

1. What message would you like to convey about who you are and what you stand for? How are you currently being represented on your current social media platforms? List the changes you can make to increase your likeability with a signature message

Cultivating Your IT Factor

that is consistent with what you want others to know about you and your business.

2. Dedicate your time to work on 1-2 social platforms in the next 30 days to increase your online visibility and likeability, infusing your signature style to differentiate you from others who have the same or similar business concept.

3. Create a plan for how you will attract your ideal audience to create social proof by engaging your ideal customers and clients to build credibility that will lead to growing your business.

4. Create a plan for your personal development to help you navigate the social platforms to create your brand awareness so you can infuse a memorable and lasting impact on the people you want to serve in your business.

Cherri

13

Must Have Principle:

Leverage IQ

FAMIRA M. GREEN

Opportunity here, opportunity there, opportunity everywhere! Every day we are presented with opportunities; they are everywhere we look. The only two questions that you have to ask yourself are: Will you see the opportunity, and will you be in a position to leverage the opportunity once you see it? There it is.

Someone has stepped into your space and given you the opportunity that you have been waiting for. It has the potential to change your ENTIRE life!

This one opportunity awaiting you that could be the difference between maintaining a lifestyle of mediocrity or achieving the lifestyle of all your dreams.

Cultivating Your IT Factor

There are four things that you must consider with every opportunity you are presented with: ***elaborate***, ***exchange***, ***equity***, and ***evolution***.

It takes vision to see the opportunity and discernment to recognize when the opportunity is right for you. Now that an opportunity has presented itself, the first step in leveraging that opportunity is to **ELABORATE**.

In the elaboration phase, you want to find out everything about the opportunity.

- Ask yourself some questions:

- What is included?

- What is necessary to get the most from the opportunity?

- What is your ultimate goal in participating in the opportunity?

There should be strategy in everything you do in business, so that your efforts are not empty and without substance. Gone are the days of jumping in head first without a plan in place.

Now let me clarify that statement for the people reading and saying to themselves,

"Some of my best results have come from jumping in without a plan." When I say that those days are gone, I'm really referring to the attitude of no responsibility that often went with that statement and action. Many times people jump into opportunities with no thought behind it, and then, when it goes bad, due to that lack, no one takes responsibility for it.

I truly believe in trusting your gut for what you should and shouldn't participate in. However, I also understand the importance of planning and strategizing in everything you do. This is where being a right-brain creative that follows her intuition, while equally being a left-brain analytic with the ability to strategize puts me at an advantage. So pull from my strength and make sure that you elaborate on the opportunities. It will be for your best, if you heed this advice. So once you have done your due diligence, what comes next?

Next, you must determine the **EXCHANGE** in the opportunity. And no, I am not talking money, at least not yet! The exchange I am referring to refers to what you have to be willing to give for the opportunity, and what you deem is the minimum you expect and are willing to receive from. For example, is it going to be a mutually beneficial exchange for all those involved in the opportunity?

When cultivating your signature brand, it is important to remain balanced in your giving as well as in your receiving. Too often, people find themselves leaning more on one side than the other. If you are leaning too much toward that of a giver, then you do not fully receive the reward of the opportunity; you find yourself burned out and possibly bitter when it's finished. On the other hand, if you are too much of a receiver, then you diminish the impact of the opportunity because you are seen as a taker with no concern for others.

Is the exchange going to make or break the worth of the opportunity? Just because it is a good opportunity does not make it a great opportunity for you.

Does this opportunity align with your brand message and your brand style? You must decide on these in the exchange phase. To partake of an opportunity, no matter how good, which does not align with your brand, can cause long-term damage. It is better to be choosy when moving forward with opportunities—each one you partake in is a direct reflection of you and your brand. Remember that fact when determining which opportunities to leverage.

Now is the time to ensure that the exchange is truly at DIVA standards. You did not think I'd speak on opportunities without bringing out the DIVA in me as well as in YOU? No, you could not have thought that!

What questions should you ask yourself to ensure that the DIVA standards are being met? Ask yourself:

1. Does this opportunity align with the **D**efinition of your destiny and the pursuit of your purpose?

2. Does this opportunity cause you to be more **I**ntriguing to your target audience?

3. Does this opportunity tap into the **V**ision that you have for building your legacy?

4. Does this opportunity make you **A**spire to keep living your life as the Diamond DIVA you are?

If you can answer yes to all four of these questions, you know that the exchange rate on this opportunity is worth moving forward.

Next up for consideration in leveraging opportunities is the **EQUITY** that you will receive from the opportunity. By equity, I am referring to income, impact, and increase.

When working toward leveraging opportunities presented to you, especially those in business, these three things are critical! What is the income potential of this opportunity? Too often, people do not want to talk the dollars and the cents. Trust me, I used to be one of those very people, never asking what the financial outcome of the opportunity was projected to be, or asking for what I wanted and deserved.

However, I heard several trusted coaches say, "Without revenue in your business, you simply have an expensive hobby." This is what changed my mindset. I do not know about you, but I am not putting all this time and effort into a hobby masquerading as a business.

My brand is to be a lucrative one so I can do what has been placed in my heart to change the world.

Just as income is important, so is the impact that this opportunity will have on your brand messaging as well as on those whom your message reaches. Let's be honest, people are not flocking to Starbucks every morning, spending $8 on a cup of coffee or tea because they are expecting mediocrity. No, they are expecting a brand that has a high level of impact on them from the service to the product. They are paying for the complete experience that Starbucks has created for them. With Starbucks releasing their 2014 Fiscal Year End Net Revenue at $4.2 billion (as reported at http://investor.starbucks.com/), it is safe to say they understand the importance of brand impact!

Is your opportunity going to increase or decrease the impact of your brand?

Lastly, when considering equity, you must determine how much, if any, increase the opportunity will bring to not only your business, but to your life. Increase can come in several forms: financial growth, personal or business growth, and spiritual growth. In everything we do, we should be looking to grow as a person. What decreases us should be cut off. How can you have a signature brand while consistently operating in opportunities of decrease?

While viewing opportunities, always view them with an insight of abundance and not from a place of lack. Too many people live their life with a scarcity mindset. Do not be one of those people. This is the evolution of your opportunity.

Elaborate....check!

Exchange....check!

Equity....check!

Now it is time to review the **EVOLUTION** of the opportunity. I know you are probably thinking to yourself, "What is she talking about the evolution of the opportunity?" When reviewing the evolution of an opportunity, it means to not only look at the long-term influence of the opportunity, but also at how the opportunity can evolve into more opportunities in the future. This is where true leverage comes into play. You are then able to take one opportunity and multiply it into several separate opportunities of the same or increased value.

Learn to see past the singleness of the current opportunity. Do not be shortsighted in your view of what is to come! Cast your net wide! If you can't see the additional opportunities for yourself, then connect with others that can help you to mastermind your opportunity and show the potential that lies within. Masterminding is a powerful tool that, when used properly, can catapult your current opportunity into the stratosphere.

Masterminding is how you can take an opportunity to speak at an event and watch it evolve into a signature speech, into a signature program, into a signature product, and into a signature brand. I personally choose to view every opportunity that I have decided is right for me and my brand as a caterpillar with the potential to metamorphose into a beautiful butterfly with no boundaries for how high or how far it can fly!

When you tap into the thought process of other thought leaders, you are able to leverage into a completely different dimension!

The definition of leverage is "the power to influence a person or situation to achieve a particular outcome." Another definition of leverage is "to use (something) to maximum advantage." That is the true magic in leveraging an opportunity: to see it blossom into something of influence that you can use to its maximum advantage!

When you take the time to go through these four steps when approaching opportunities, there are also some side effects, so to speak, that you can't help but notice. Building relationships is one of those side effects. As you cultivate the opportunity, you will build the relationships that are attached to that opportunity. This is often the pivot into evolving opportunities into bigger and better for those open to it.

Clearer vision is another side effect of truly understanding the art of leveraging your opportunities. Your vision for your brand and destiny becomes clearer as you evaluate opportunities to see if they truly align with who and what you want. Often this process will help you become laser focused, because you'll find that what you thought you wanted or needed you actually don't. This was the case for me on several occasions.

For example, when I was presented with opportunities to be a co-author in two separate book projects at the same time, this process actually helped me to narrow my vision. This ended up revealing that the opportunities I thought would be the perfect fit for me actually weren't based on the narrowed and more focused vision for my brand.

Allow yourself to see clearer with every opportunity presented to you. Embrace being uniquely you, and know that you have the right and the authority to pick and choose the opportunities you want to be a part of, as well as those you want to leverage into other things. Don't be afraid to tell people, "That sounds like a wonderful opportunity; however, it is not one that I plan to pursue at this time." There is nothing wrong with that statement.

Your brand will be better for the opportunities you say yes to, and your brand will be better for the opportunities you say no to. Being selective is a skill and a positive move for you to make. Just as any drink loses its flavor once watered down, the same can be said about the flavor of your brand when you jump at every opportunity presented to you.

When you operate from this place of truth, you are leveraging your opportunities with style. Style is always important because it's the style and grace in which you operate that makes you memorable to potential collaborators, clients, and customers. As you cultivate the opportunities that you pursue, the more opportunities will be drawn to you, and it will be the right opportunities to enhance your brand.

BIG to increase their financial bottom line by creating a signature style with a LOOK that gets them BOOKED and renders them unforgettable, allowing them to achieve all the success they are destined for!

Famira

14

Must Have Principle:

Time Management

TONEIKA SHERROD

As entrepreneurs and success seekers, you tend to have many obligations, goals, and creative ideas. The problem normally lies within these three things with regards to managing your time. Right now, you are trying to reach a level of success that can only be reached if you take the proper steps. One of those steps is to learn to manage your time and the activities spent with it. To build a powerhouse brand, it is vital to know how to take advantage of every minute of your day while producing effectively.

Here, you will learn how to manage your time and still be able to juggle all your titles. You will also gain more confidence in reaching your goals and performing effectively.

Cultivating Your IT Factor

At this point in your life, you are trying to build your signature brand. No matter what your brand is, you will need the time to put into it. Branding can be time consuming if your time is not properly managed. As I stated before, you have obligations that may take a lot of your time.

To list a few: You could have children to care for, businesses to run, a husband or wife to give attention to, a ministry to grow and maintain, a job to work, and let's not forget the most important thing—a relationship with God that you must grow and spend time on. If I did not mention your obligation, just place it on the list.

All of these are big responsibilities, and if you don't manage them correctly, they can create frustration, stress, discouragement, doubt, procrastination, and even withdrawal.

Make Every Second Count:

You may have heard this many times, but I'm going to say it again because it's true: Time is one of your most valued assets in life. You don't like people wasting your time, and you definitely don't want to waste your own time and other's. This could be applied in all aspects of your life. Everyone has the same amount of hours in a day. With twenty-four hours in a day, you have to make all 1,440 minutes count. I will simplify it for you. Mostly all of our days are organized by activities or routines. During these activities or routines, there are some gaps in time where you are not doing anything.

For example, you might need to wash clothes, which could take up to 1-3 hours of your day, depending on how many loads you have. Between cycles, you are able to multi-task and get one or two more tasks checked off your list.

Now you have just created more time for other tasks. If you do this every day, then you should get everything you need to get done while having extra time to build your brand. From this day forth, pay more attention to time you spend on activities and which activities you give your time to.

As you pay more attention, make adjustments to your schedule as needed to make sure every activity has a purpose. Your goal is to manage your time while working effectively. Doing both of these will increase your rate of success.

See the Bigger Picture:

I love to look at the bigger picture in every situation. In this one, you will be looking at the bigger picture of time management, which gives you a view of the end results from your actions. This will help you understand how managing your time helps motivate you and keep you focused on why you are doing what you are doing. I want you to close your eyes and picture an accomplishment that you are trying to reach. Now see yourself already there. You should feel the emotions of excitement, happiness, and relief. Doesn't this give you a push to work toward this accomplishment?

You may be asking, "What does the end result have to do with managing my time?" Well, if you know what you are working toward, then you have an urgency to get it done in the timeframe you are expecting, and you won't waste time on activities that don't push you to that goal.

You will also know which activities to give attention to. Perfecting your skills in time management will lead to success in all areas of your life. It will take pressure off, put you in a more peaceful and rejuvenated state mentally and physically, give you a boost of confidence in your own unique abilities, improve your health, and provide you with opportunities for higher success.

Assignment:

Here's how to take your goal (whether short term or long term) and break it down into daily tasks, which will help you reach your goal without frustration or burn out.

Take one of your goals and write out daily or weekly tasks that can lead to the completion.

Example:

Goal: To write and publish my book in six months.

Weekly/Daily Tasks:

1. Write for one hour a day.

2. Search for a publisher.

3. Put $450-500 away every month for publishing.

This is just an example. The goal is to make it as simple as possible for you to get this done in the time you have. You can break these tasks down as much as you need to.

Scenario:

You are a busy mom and wife, work a 9-5 job, and are an entrepreneur in transition. Your obligations are clouding your mind and life, and you don't know how to manage all of this and keep everyone satisfied. I am going to cover each obligation separately so you can understand the end result. As a mom, your children demand your attention and have their own activities. This is great!

When your children are at their activities, you can get some things done. This is where having your task list available will come in handy. Pick a task that you can complete in the time you are waiting for your children. The end result is you get what you need to get done, and your children are happy because they made it to their activity and you are there to support them.

Let's move to the next obligation. As a wife, your husband demands a lot of attention from you (if not, then even better). Get what you need to get done for your husband. Give your husband the attention he requires and leave your tasks for when you have satisfied your husband. You may need to work during late hours when everyone is asleep (I never said you wouldn't work late). It may help also to explain to your husband your goals and your daily tasks so he will understand and be supportive, so let him know what the end result will be; this helps to sell the importance of your activities.

Let's move on to the next obligation. Working a 9-5 can be tiring and time consuming, but if you change your mindset, it won't be that tiring. Look at it as though you are working temporarily to fund your dream. Minus the eight hours of sleep, you only have the eight hours to work with. Use the multi-tasking strategy and get more than one thing done at a time. For example, wash clothes while writing for 30 minutes to one hour for your book. When working eight hours to 12 hours a day, you have to pick your tasks carefully and make every second count. The last obligation is the most time consuming, but it's also the most manageable.

An entrepreneur in transition is a hard but rewarding obligation. It takes organization and planning to be successful at this goal. At first you should spend your time with making a plan for success. Once you have done this, things should get a little easier. It is the planning that takes the most time and work. You have heard that if you build something on a solid and fertile ground, then it will grow strong and will last.

Tip: Keep it simple! The frustration that comes from trying to manage your time is the result of the complexity of your thoughts when you are trying to process too much at one time. If you practice this, it will be easier for you to manage your time, and you will have room left for extra activities.

Commonly asked questions:

1. **Why is time management so important?**

    Answer: Time is an asset of life that only comes once. It is not repeatable or transferable. You only get one opportunity to make the best out of every second in your life. No one knows when her time is up, so make every moment count.

2. **How can I master my time?**

    Answer: I'm not going to say mastering your time is easy, but it is simple. As for anything you are trying to master, you have to practice. Practice makes progress. Eventually, you will be doing it without effort.

3. **What are some techniques to help me master my time?**

    Answer: Well, I gave you one technique in the assignment above, but here are a few more: Have a plan, know the obstacles that may stop you on the journey, have a back-up plan, know your priorities, keep track of your time spent on all activities, don't waste your or other's time, and work effectively and on purpose. These are just some examples to help you get started.

4. **How can I make sure that I am managing my time right?**

    Answer: To know if you are effectively managing your time, you will need to have a visual tracker (like written out goals or a chart) that can help you track your progress. That's why it is important to write out your goals.

If you don't track your goals, how can you know if you have achieved them? This is the most effective way to make sure you are managing your time right. You will also know if you are seeing the fruit of your labor. What does "seeing the fruit of your labor" mean? If you are seeing the results of what you are doing, then you are making progress and managing your activities and time correctly.

5. How do I know if I am not spending the right time on something?

Answer: You will know if you are wasting your time or if you need to put more time into an activity. If you are wasting your time, you will know this sooner than if you need to put more time into the activity. If an activity is not going to get you to where you need to be, then you don't need to spend any time on it.

If you are not producing fruit or making progress on an activity, then you may need to spend the same amount of time on it but change what you are doing.

Sometimes you have to change the way you do something to make it produce fruit. (Hint: You don't necessarily need to spend more time on an activity, just change what you are doing during the activity.)

Toneika

Author Bios ...

• STEVII AISHA MILLS •

Stevii Aisha Mills empowers women to live out their gifts in an extraordinary way by tapping into their God-Given It Factor.

Holding a Bachelor of Arts Degree in Public Relations and a Master's of Science Degree in Human Resources from North Carolina A&T State University, she is able to align and execute visions, concepts, motivational products, speaking engagements and workshops for women who are dedicated to using network marketing opportunity as a platform to brand themselves and launch their dreams.

She is the founder of the B.E.A.U.T.Y. Queen Society, and currently serves as the Marketing Chairperson for the Special Events Ministry at Destiny Christian Center. She connects with her audience regularly via her "Just Stevii" podcast and writing column.

To learn more about Stevii visit:
www.Stevii.com

• VERNA V. NICKLEBERRY •

Ms. Verna V. Nickelberry, mother of two sons and the grandmother of two little boys, Zion Truth Oliver and Israel Jadon Oliver, is a graduate of Northside High School and LeMoyne-Owen College located in Memphis, Tennessee. Ms. Nickelberry has completed classes toward a masters degree in theology at Jacksonville Theological Seminary.

Ms. Nickelberry is the founder and editorial director of *Ordinary People Magazine* (OPM). Ordinary People Magazine is the result of a God-given assignment that Ms. Nickelberry received in 2005, although it wasn't created until March of 2008.

Ms. Nickelberry has given many hours of services to others. Her servant's heart can be seen in her work as the visionary of (OPM).

• DEBRAYTA (DEE) SALLEY •

Abundant Life Coach, Debrayta (Dee) Salley is compassionate, fun loving, resilient, and God-fearing. She enjoys writing, reading, and hosting wellness events. She has a son and resides in Maryland.

After becoming a certified life coach in October, 2010, Ms. Salley began nurturing her gift and passion for writing as a tool to provide resources for others who are interested in developing both personally and spiritually. Her writings are birthed from a place of experience and compassion under the direction of the Holy Spirit. She helps others unlock the hidden places of life and draws them into the Lord's light for rejuvenation. Ms. Salley has accepted her assignment to provide resources of encouragement to help others make conscious decisions that will render their best life experiences.

Connect with Debrayta by visiting:
www.DeeAbundantLifeCoach.com or via email at dee_abundantlifecoach@yahoo.com

• M.E. PORTER •

M.E. Porter is the CEO of ME Unlimited LLC, a faith-based coaching and personal development organization, and the founder of Motivationally ME, the ministry of motivation.

She is a dynamic speaker and teacher, seasoned mentor, spiritual adviser, and life coach. M.E.

is known to rock her audiences at the core as she speaks about authentic soul-filled living, healthy emotions and spirituality, positioning and purpose, and more. Her audience includes business, secular, and spiritual groups, and individuals seeking joy, wholeness, and inner freedom.

To learn more or to book M.E. visit:
www.MarilynEPorter.com
Facebook/ IamMEPorter
Twitter @MEMotivates
email: info@marilyneporter.com
call: 404-500-8722

• FUNGAI NDEMERA •

Fungai is an award-winning entrepreneur, mentor, business strategist, and motivational coach with more than 15 years of experience in business leadership. She motivates and teaches others the process of branding and building a business from scratch to seven-figures while creating the lives they dream of. She believes that the only way to enjoy freedom and have a successful empire is to build a powerful brand that supports systems and structures.

Coming from poverty in Zimbabwe to creating a thriving, socially conscious seven-figure business in the United Kingdom, she encourages others to live their dreams by sharing her own story and breaking through their fears. After experiencing the highs and lows of business, she has found her mission, which is supporting female entrepreneurs on their own paths. Her guide, *How I Created a 7-Figure Business from Scratch*, is being offered as a free e-book at www.FungaiNdemera.com

• RHONDA McALISTER •

Rhonda McAlister has been working with clients who have been seeking her entrepreneurial vision since 2012. Rhonda has combined her love and talent for assisting and mentoring others, along with her background in business, to launch Rhonda's Workshops & Events.

Rhonda's Workshops & Events mission is to deliver her message of Mindset Motivation. A combination of motivational and business mindset talks to understand our thought processes and how they determine the present and future state of our revenue models.

She is a contributing writer for the book *Confession of a Welfare Mom, Vol. 1,* and the author of *To Become A Successful Entrepreneur, You Must Develop A Habit Of...*, *Crossover: A Tale of Twin Brothers Living In Separate Worlds* and *Crossover II*. For those wanting to learn from home, she released her first e-course Business + Mindset = The Essential Package, along with the workbook.

Connect with Rhonda by visiting:
www.ItsMissRhonda.com

• CYNETA HILL •

A servant of God, Cyneta Hill is someone who has fallen and gotten back up. A person who cares about the well being of others. Someone who believes that she can do all things through Jesus Christ who strengthens her. Someone who endured a lot on her journey to living personally and professionally.

By God's grace and mercy in the light of academic vision was shined upon her, leading her to pursue a career as an occupational therapist. As a result of her academic vision, *Graceful In Home Aging* came into fruition, a community-based healthcare service that assists aging persons, persons with physical disabilities, and caregivers in order to enhance their quality of life. Cyneta also enjoys giving back to her community, which leads to her working closely with the Dress For Success organization, and the Office of Public Guardian.

• LISA WILSON •

Lisa Wilson, Inspired Wealth & Business Coach, is a successful Money Market expert who has been instrumental in managing multi-million dollar portfolios with a top-rated investment and banking firm during her 20-year corporate career.

Lisa has made it her mission to share the importance of money management and the ways to enjoy financial well being by applying the *"Roadmap for Wealth Strategies."* Lisa is fully committed to your personal growth and development as she shares her winning spirit and powerful techniques.

Cultivating Your IT Factor

• MINISTER NILLIE WOSU •

Minister Wosu is a national spokesperson for *WomenHeart: The National Coalition for Women with Heart Disease*. Nellie is also a patient spokesperson for the national health agenda *Measure Up Pressure Down*.

Wosu was referenced in an article in the March 2013 Edition of ESSENCE Magazine concerning stress's impact on today's woman. Also, in December 2012, Wosu penned her journey with heart disease entitled, *The Keeper of Me*, an Amazon bestseller, published by Gatmoon Publishing, L.L.C. of which she is the publisher & CEO.

Minister Wosu resides in Concord, North Carolina, and has one daughter, Summer Wosu. Nellie Wosu is not only surviving with heart disease, she is thriving, and she encourages others to do the same with their own health journeys. In fact, Nellie believes that the disease has propelled her towards her life's mission and purpose for His glory, which is to benefit many, perhaps even you!

• MISTE M. ANDERS–CLEMONS •

Life Coach, Miste M. Anders-Clemons, also known as "The Stress Strategist," and founder of It's a Misteism, has been working with people for over 20 years in teaching and training. She has a commitment to helping people reach their full potential and personal goals. Her specialties are: stress reduction, life transitions, empowerment, goal planning, and movement.

As a second-degree black belt in Shotokan karate, a teacher of Tai Chi Chuan (Yang Style), former All-American in track and field, and as a Hula and Tahitian dancer, life coach Miste draws from these life experiences and disciplines to educate, teach, and enrich other's lives and use them as the basis for her inspirational speaking and life coaching.

Connect with Miste by visiting:
www.Misteism.com
email: miste@misteism.com
call: (682) 521-5908

• ALAINA ODESSA •

Alaina Odessa is "The Christian Meditation & Mind Renewal Maven." She's also the founder of Born Again Women in BLOOM, a ministry on a mission to use ancient and creative tools to educate, empower and enrich the lives of Christian women who are ready to search their hearts and renew their minds so that they can BLOOM into being the fully expressed, fulfilled and free vessels of Love, Light and Radiance they were created by God to be.

She is a writer, spoken word artist, poet, actress, word lover and author of the anointed collection of poetry, *Slow Running Honey and First Born Poems of Salvation*.

Alaina loves to travel and is available for speaking engagements, workshops, spoken word performances, and public appearances for large and intimate audiences.

To learn more, or to book her or your next event, visit www.AlainaO.com.

Author Bios

• CHERRI WALSTON •

Cherri Walston, "The BIG Vision Mentor" and the CEO of Big Vision Biz, LLC, is passionate about helping professional and aspiring women entrepreneurs create a vibrant vision for their exit strategy so they can move forward with confidence, courage, and freedom to build their passion business beyond their 9 to 5 job.

Cherri is very skillful at helping professional women articulate their passionate life's vision. She also leads them to create a soul-fulfilling business that aligns with their personal missions. In addition, she guides her clients in making the transition from employee to entrepreneur with a strategic plan of action for building a business while working a full-time job.

Cherri is the author of HER Exit Strategy: *The Working Woman's Freedom Plan to Live Your Big Vision.*

Connect with Cherri by visiting: www.BigVisionMentor.com or send an email to cherri@bigvisionmentor

• FAMIRA M. GREEN •

Famira M. Green is "The Diamond DIVA." She's also known as The Style Translator™. Her life's mission is to work with women and help them learn to share their authentic #BeautyOUTLoud!

She's Chief Visionary Officer of Diamond DIVA International, a full service, boutique-style image and visual coaching business. She shows women how to create a vibrant signature style to be an unforgettable showstopper. She empowers women to translate their style desires and play BIG to increase their financial bottom line by creating a signature style with a LOOK that gets them BOOKED and renders them unforgettable, allowing them to achieve all the success they are destined for.

Famira is an international bestselling author, speaker, and thought leader. Famira currently resides in Hampton, Virginia, and is an avid traveler. She is a servant leader, affectionately called the Empress of Empowerment.

Connect with Famira online at:
www.FamiraGreen.com
Facebook/ DiamondDIVAfg

• TONEIKA SHERROD •

Toneika Amelia Sherrod is a dynamic wife and mother. She is known for her experience and intelligence in personal and spiritual growth. In addition, she is an author, mentor, and dream to reality/spiritual life coach, and empowerment speaker who is respected for her love and service to others.

Toneika is the CEO/Founder of Anointed Dream Building LLC and is also the host of Success Talk. She invites other professionals to share her platform and speak to her audience to add to her knowledge on various subjects.

She helps bring dreams to reality for those willing to take immediate action and take accountability for their work.

Connect with Toneika online at:
Facebook/ Anointed Dream Building
Facebook/ Toneika Sherrod
Twitter @ToneikaSherrod
YouTube, Instagram, Google+, LinkedIn, and Spreaker: ToneikaSherrod
email: TTdreambuilding@gmail.com
call: 919-307-5081

WE WANT TO HEAR FROM YOU!!!

If this book has made a difference in your life Stevii would be delighted to hear about it.

Leave a review on Amazon.com!

BOOK STEVII TO SPEAK AT YOUR NEXT EVENT!

Send an email to booking@publishyourgift.com
Learn more about Stevii at
www.Stevii.com

• • • • •

FOLLOW STEVII ON SOCIAL MEDIA

  SteviiAishaMills   SteviiMills

"EMPOWERING YOU TO IMPACT GENERATIONS"
WWW.PUBLISHYOURGIFT.COM

www.ingramcontent.com/pod-product-compliance
Lightning Source LLC
Chambersburg PA
CBHW071614080526
44588CB00010B/1131